D1789337

READINGS
IN
CONTEMPORARY
CULTURE

Alice S. Horning

Department of English
Wayne State University

McGraw-Hill

New York   St. Louis   San Francisco   Auckland   Beirut   Bogotá   Düsseldorf
Johannesburg   Kuala Lumpur   London   Madrid   Mexico   Montreal   New Delhi
Panama   Paris   San Juan   São Paulo   Singapore   Sydney   Tokyo   Toronto

Editorial Development: Winifred Davis
Editing Supervisor: Annette Koshut
Design: Pat Friedman
Production: Robert C. Pedersen

Library of Congress Cataloging in Publication Data

Horning, Alice S.
Readings in contemporary culture.

    SUMMARY: Includes readings on 25 topics of contemporary interest accompanied by comprehension and writing exercises for intermediate level students of English as a foreign language.
    1. English language—Text-books for foreigners.
2. Readers—United States. [1. English language—
Textbooks for foreigners] I. Title.
PEll28.H56   428'.6'4   78-31136
ISBN 0-07-030352-5
Copyright © 1979 by McGraw-Hill, Inc.

ISBN 0-07-030352-5

1234567890   D O D O   78765432109

Contents

ACKNOWLEDGMENTS

I would like to thank the following people for their help with the preparation of the manuscript of this book: Dr. Margo Goldman of the Massachusetts General Hospital, Boston, provided critical readings of the chapters on medicine; Mr. Malcolm Smith, President of Macromatic, Incorporated, Chicago, provided helpful background on the international money market, and directed me to useful sources on the subject; Ms. Kathy Zamora of the English department at Wayne State University, Detroit, typed the manuscript quickly and accurately. Errors and omissions that remain are, of course, mine alone.

PREFACE

This text is for students of English as a second language who wish to develop their skills in reading. The style of the essays encourages the reader to get meaning from the text itself without relying on a dictionary or the glossary. Hence, the text is deliberately somewhat repetitive in style. Readers who are just beginning to read extended passages of English prose will find these readings interesting, and will build their vocabulary and comprehension skills at the same time.

There are a variety of exercises for classroom use. In each chapter, comprehension questions check a reader's understanding of content. Two types of discussion questions are given. Part A questions are relatively simple. They invite the reader to talk about ideas discussed in the reading. Part B questions are more challenging, raising issues indirectly related to the essay. Readers are asked to show their understanding of the vocabulary of each chapter by creating directed sentences using combinations of the new words introduced in the chapter. Beginning readers should be asked to use each item alone in a sentence, or to use combinations of only two vocabulary items per sentence. More advanced readers will be able to follow the directions given. Readers who have difficulty understanding new vocabulary will find glossaries by chapter at the back of the book.

Every fifth chapter is a review chapter. It introduces no new vocabulary and has no glossary. Unlike the other essays, which are expository, the review chapters consist of opinion essays. These essays will help readers distinguish between the presentation of facts and the presentation of opinions. The comprehension and discussion questions following the opinion papers focus the reader's attention on finding and understanding the writer's views. These review chapters conclude with a word study exercise which explains common prefixes and suffixes in English, using as examples vocabulary introduced in previous chapters. A short usage practice follows the explanation.

Additional readings on the topic of each essay are also given: books, magazines and newspapers are cited for readers interested in reading more on a topic, and for those wanting to practice and expand their reading abilities.

HIGHER EDUCATION IN THE UNITED STATES

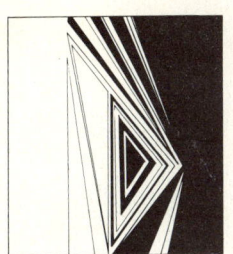

In the United States, a student who has finished high school may want to continue in higher education. There are several ways to continue in higher education in the United States. There are universities, colleges, community colleges, and technical or vocational schools. Each of these kinds of higher education will be described below.

A university is much larger than a college. It is larger for two reasons. First, a university in the United States usually has several different colleges in it. Each college within the university has a special subject area. There may be a college of liberal arts where humanities, social science, natural science, and mathematics are taught. There may be a college of education where students learn to be teachers. There may be a college of business where business subjects are taught. All of these colleges may be part of one university. Sometimes, in a university, each college is called a "school": "The School of Liberal Arts," "The School of Business," or "The School of Education." Second, the university always has programs for advanced or graduate study in a variety of subjects. There may be a medical school, a law school, and other advanced programs.

Students in the United States must have a high school diploma or its equivalent, to enter one of the colleges in the university. Most students have completed regular high school programs. Some older students may have the same amount of education even though they have not completed high school. These students have the equivalent of a high school degree. University students may study for an undergraduate degree in the arts or sciences. If they complete a course of study in the arts, they receive bachelor of arts degrees. In the sciences, they receive bachelor of science degrees. Students may leave the university at this time, or they may choose to go on for a graduate or professional degree.

The university may get money for its expenses from several different sources. It may get some money from the state government. If so, it is a publicly funded university. The university may get money only from private sources: contributions, tuition, investments, and other sources. If this is the case, it is a privately funded university. Finally, a university may be funded by a religious group.

Hunter College, New York City

A university program for undergraduates usually takes four years. In this way, a university and a college are alike. College students usually spend four years in school also. A college, however, usually has only one or two kinds of programs. A college does not have graduate or professional programs in a variety of areas.

A college is also like a university in the kinds of students it has. College students, like university students, usually have a high school diploma when they enter college. If a college student completes a course of study in the arts, he or she receives a bachelor of arts degree. In the sciences, the students receive a bachelor of science degree. If college students want to continue for a graduate or professional degree, they must go to a university.

The college is usually funded in one of the three ways already described. It may be publicly or privately funded. Or, it may be funded by a religious group.

Compared to universities and colleges, community colleges in the United States are quite different. The program of study in the community college usually lasts only two years. Many different subjects are taught in the community college. Not all of the subjects are the usual school subjects. The community college may give courses in dental technology, auto mechanics, sewing, and many other nonacademic subjects. The community college may also have courses in the regular academic subjects like science, math, languages, literature, and other courses in the humanities.

Many different types of students study at community colleges. Not all students have a high school diploma. Many students are adults with children, and sometimes with grandchildren, of their own. The community college serves the community, and anyone who lives nearby may go. When community college students complete a two-year program, they receive an associate of arts or associate of science degree. They may then go to a college or university for two more years to get the bachelor's degree. However, the student may get a job instead, or just stop going to school.

Community colleges are nearly always publicly funded, by the state, county, or city governments. They are not usually funded by religious groups.

The community college gives training for a variety of jobs, and also has an academic program. The technical or vocational school, however, has only job training. Its programs may last a short time or a long time. Some programs take six months, while other programs may take two years or more to complete.

Students in the technical or vocational school may have a high school diploma. Many, however, do not have the diploma. Many people go to a technical or vocational school instead of going to high school. When they complete their training, they may be able to get a good job right away. The technical or vocational school provides training for work in areas such as electronics, carpentry, plumbing, and others.

The technical or vocational school may be funded in any of the ways already described. It may be publicly or privately funded, or it may be funded by a religious group. Other sources of money for this kind of school are trade unions or charity organizations.

Students who have finished high school, and even some who do not go to high school, may choose from these four kinds of higher education in the United States. High school students who want further academic or professional training may go to a college or university. Students who want both academic and nonacademic training may go to the community college. Students who want to learn a job may go to a technical or vocational school. Students may choose the kind of higher education that they like best.

EXERCISES
Comprehension
1. What are the four kinds of higher education described in the essay?
2. What is a university?
3. How does the university get money for its expenses?
4. Who may go to a university?
5. How long does it take to get an undergraduate degree?
6. Give three ways in which a college and a university are alike.
7. How do community colleges differ from universities and colleges?
8. Describe the community college student.
9. Compare the community college to a technical or vocational school.
10. What are some subjects you could study at a technical or vocational school?

Cornell University

Cornell University, Ithaca, New York

Discussion

Part A

1. What do students in your country do when they finish high school?
2. Do very many students continue to study after high school?
3. What are the different kinds of schools you can go to after high school?
4. Must you finish high school before going on to another kind of school?
5. Can anyone continue to go to school after high school?
6. How do students in your country pay for their education after high school?
7. Compare the kinds of funding in United States higher education with the funding in your country.

Part B

1. Compare United States higher education to higher education in your country. Which do you like best? Why?
2. If you were a United States citizen, which kind of higher education would you choose? Why?
3. If you are in the United States or plan to go there to study, which kind of higher education would you choose? Why?
4. Read the catalog of a United States university, college, community college, or technical or vocational school. Describe one of the programs at the school.

Directed Sentences

Directions: Make sentences using the following word groups. You may use any form of a given word. You may use the words in any order.

1. electronics-carpentry-plumbing-technical or vocational school-others
2. auto mechanics-dental technology-sewing-community college
3. higher education-described-essay
4. diploma-associate degree-however
5. undergraduate degree-bachelor's degree-equivalent
6. university-graduate-professional-enter
7. sources-expenses-private-publicly funded
8. contributions-charity organizations-trade unions-larger-investments
9. nonacademic-training-group
10. receive-liberal arts
11. tuition-amount-higher education
12. adults-grandchildren-humanities

Suggested Reading

College catalogs for U.S. colleges and universities
Profiles of American Colleges (Barron's Publishing, 1976)

Note: Turn to Glossary (page 155) for words emphasized for study in each chapter.

LINGUISTICS

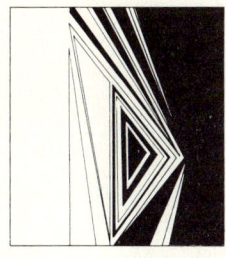 You are a student of English as a second language. This means that you do not yet know English completely. But you do know another language. This is the language that you already speak. It is sometimes called your native language. You may speak French, or Arabic, or Japanese. You can do many things with your native language. You can speak it, of course. You can also understand it. You can read it and write it too. Linguistics is a field of study that is concerned with these abilities that you have. It studies your ability to speak and understand a language—any language. Linguists are trying to understand your ability to use a language.

Much of the modern work in linguistics has been done in the United States in the last fifteen years. Noam Chomsky, an American professor of linguistics at the Massachusetts Institute of Technology, has written several important books on linguistics during this time. Chomsky and other scholars have been studying our ability to use and understand language. The linguists have been asking questions about these abilities that we all have. They have been developing a theory to explain how people can use language. The theory tries to account for four of our abilities with language.

One of your abilities with your language is your ability to speak it. You can say a sentence in your language. This is very easy for you to do. In fact, you can say many sentences in your language. If you tried to say all of the sentences in your language, however, you could not do it. Linguists know that there are an infinite number of sentences in every language. Every speaker of the language has the ability to say them all. But because there are so many possible sentences, no speaker could find the time to actually do this. Linguists are trying to explain this unused ability all speakers have to say all the sentences of their language.

A second ability that you have with your language is your ability to understand it. If someone says something to you in your native language, you will probably understand it. You can understand almost all of the sentences in your native language. All speakers of a language have the ability to understand all of the sentences of their language. They may not understand all of the words, but they can probably understand a very large number of the sentences spoken in the language.

Carola Gregor/Monkmeyer

"Chicken too hot to eat"

A third ability you have with your language is your ability to understand two different sentences which have the same meaning. You may not yet be able to do this with two sentences in English. But you can probably do it with two sentences in your native language. Here are two sentences in English: "The child wrote down the number." "The child wrote the number down." You can probably understand that these two sentences mean the same thing. If not, you may ask your teacher, or someone who knows English very well. They will tell you that these two sentences mean the same thing. You can probably make up two sentences in your native language that mean the same thing. You have the ability to understand that two different sentences may have the same meaning. All native speakers of your language will also understand that these two sentences have the same meaning. All native speakers of a language can do this. Linguists are trying to understand this ability that people have with their language.

A fourth ability that you have with your language has to do with ambiguous sentences. A sentence is ambiguous if it has more than one meaning. There are many such sentences in all languages. All speakers have the ability to understand ambiguous sentences. You can understand an ambiguous sentence in your native language. It is easy to say what two meanings the sentence has. Someone else who speaks your language will also know that the sentence is ambiguous. This person will find the same two meanings in the sentence that you find. The sentence "The chicken was too hot to eat" is ambiguous in English. If you do not understand the two meanings of the sentence, perhaps a more advanced student or a native speaker can explain them to you. You will not have this problem when you know English well, and you do not have a problem understanding ambiguous sentences in your native language. Linguists would like to know more about this ability which all native speakers have.

Chomsky and other scholars have a theory to explain these abilities that all people seem to have with language. This theory is called transformational generative grammar. Linguists believe that all people know certain things about language. Everyone knows how language works. You use this knowledge to say sentences in your native language. You also use this knowledge to understand sentences in your language. It helps you to understand two sentences that have the same meaning. The same knowledge allows you to understand the two meanings of an ambiguous sentence. Transformational theory may explain what we know when we know a language. It may make language learning easier sometime in the future. The theory has many interesting and important possibilities.

EXERCISES
Comprehension
1. What is linguistics?
2. Who is Noam Chomsky?
3. What have Chomsky and other scholars been working on?
4. Explain your first ability with language.
5. Discuss your second ability with language.

6. Do you understand the two sentences which have the same meaning? Explain.
7. What is your fourth ability with language?
8. What is an ambiguous sentence?
9. What is transformational generative grammar?
10. What may transformational theory help to explain?

Discussion

Part A

1. Would you like to be a linguist? Why or why not?
2. If you were a linguist, what areas in linguistics would you study?
3. Do you think linguists could contribute to world peace and understanding? How?
4. Should there be an international language? Should it be a new language? Your language? English? Give your view and explain it.

Part B

1. What is language?
2. How do you use it?
3. Have you ever listened to a child learn to talk? What happens? How do you think the child learns?
4. How many languages do you speak?
5. Do you know anyone who speaks many languages?
6. Is all language spoken or written?

Robert J. Capece

"Chicken too hot to eat"

Directed Sentences

Directions: Make sentences using the following word groups. You may use any form of a given word. You may use the words in any order.

1. account-ambiguous-chicken-meaning
2. linguist-concerned-ability-allow-unused
3. field-linguistics-possibility-professor-scholar
4. actually-speaker-certain-knowledge
5. believe-transformational generative grammar-theory
6. person-easier-infinite-native language

Suggested Reading

Falk, Julia S. *Linguistics and Language* (Wiley, 1978)
Fast, Julius. *Body Language* (Evans, 1970)
Hall, Edward. *The Silent Language* (Doubleday, 1973)
Lyons, John. *Chomsky* (Fontana Modern Masters, 1970)
Postman, Neil & C. Weingartner. *Linguistics* (Dell, 1966)

THE OLYMPICS

Who are Comaneci and Hammel? Tretyak and Fujimoto? They represented their countries at the 1976 Olympics. The Olympic games are an international sports competition. In the Olympics, athletes play in many different types of games. Some athletes compete in the Winter Olympics. Some compete in the Summer Olympics. The Olympic games are very old and have a very interesting history.

The first Olympic games were held in Greece in ancient times. They probably began in the sixth century, B.C. The contests were held every four years in the summer. The first games lasted for only one day. There was only one contest. It was a short race. Only Greek men were allowed to run in the race. No women were allowed, and no non-Greeks were allowed to run in the race. Women were not allowed to watch the race either, or to be anywhere near the racing area. Other events were added later. One event added later was swimming. But the ancient games were stopped in the fourth century, A.D., when Greece was ruled by Rome.

The Olympics were started again in the nineteenth century, after Baron Pierre de Coubertin, a Frenchman, suggested that it would be good to have the games again, but not just for Greek people. De Coubertin organized a meeting in 1894. Representatives from nine countries went to the meeting, in Paris. They agreed to start the Olympic games again in Athens, Greece, in 1896.

The Olympic games have been held every four years since 1896. Three times, the games were not held because of a world war. There were no games in 1916, 1940, and 1944. The first competition in modern times was held in Athens, but not all of the games have been held there. The Olympic games are held in many different cities around the world.

Baron de Coubertin also started a committee to run the Olympics. This committee is called the International Olympic Committee. It has offices in Lausanne, Switzerland. The Committee has made many decisions that affect the modern Olympics. In 1912, the Committee decided to allow women to compete. In 1924, a second group of games was begun. These new games were played in the winter of each Olympic year. In 1976, the Summer Olympics were held in Montreal, Canada, and the Winter Olympics were held in Innsbruck, Austria.

United Press International

Comenici

The International Olympic Committee makes the rules for athletes in the Olympics. These rules are very strict. (1) Everyone who would like to be in the Olympics must be an amateur. This means that the athletes must not get any money for playing a sport. They must not have played the sport professionally. (2) There are no age limits. An athlete can be young or old. (3) No one can be kept out of the Olympics because of religion, color, or political ideas. This rule means that athletes from all countries can compete. (4) Only people who were born in a particular country can represent that country in the games. (5) The Committee also says that in each event, each country can have only three entries in the summer games, and four entries in the winter. These rules help to make sure that everyone has the same chance to win.

The events and games are of several different types. There are individual contests, where each athlete plays alone. To win this type of contest, one athlete must be better, faster, or stronger than other athletes. Some examples of individual games are swimming, running, and walking races. These events happen in the summer. Some winter events are skiing and sledding races. Some other individual events are jumping, gymnastics, and diving.

In a second group of events and games, three or four athletes work as a group. These contests are usually races, and the fastest group wins. For these small groups, there are relay races in running and swimming in summer, and relays in skiing in winter.

In a third group of games, teams from each country compete in sports. To win these games, one team must have a higher score than the other team. The athletes must usually be able to catch, throw, hit, or kick a ball very well to win. For teams, there are many kinds of games. The teams play games such as basketball, soccer, and volleyball.

For an amateur athlete, winning in the Olympics is a great achievement. The games are not easy to win, whether an athlete competes in the summer or in the winter. There are many excellent athletes who compete alone, in small groups, or on teams. An athlete who wins the Olympics is the best in the world.

EXERCISES

Comprehension

1. Describe the first Olympic games.
2. When were they played, and where?
3. Why did the games stop?
4. How did the Olympics begin again?
5. Who is the Baron de Coubertin?
6. Explain the rules for athletes in the Olympics now.
7. Describe the three types of contests.
8. Name some summer games.
9. Name some winter games.
10. Explain what winning in the Olympics means.

Sovfoto

Tretyak

Discussion

Directions: Answer questions in part A and part B if your country plays in the Olympics. Answer questions in part B if your country does not play in the Olympics.

Part A

1. What events does your country compete in?
2. Name some of the people on your Olympic team if you can.
3. If your team wins in the Olympics, how are the athletes received when they come home?
4. How important are the Olympic games in your country?

Part B

1. What is your view of international sports competition? Do you think it is good or bad?
2. Are the Olympics too political now?
3. Do you like to play sports more than to watch them? Why?
4. Describe some sports you like to play or watch.
5. If you do not like sports, explain your point of view.

Directed Sentences

Directions: Make sentences using the following word groups. You may use any form of a given word. You may use the words in any order.

1. suggested-chance-achievements
2. decisions-committee-strict-athletes
3. events-affect-history-political
4. types-sports-competition-mentioned

5. skiing-jumping-soccer-gymnastics-volleyball
6. meeting-century-times
7. excellent-individual-represented
8. relay-score-stronger-win
9. entries-limits-contests
10. greatest-amateur-race
11. catch-hit-kick

Suggested Reading

Durant, John. *Highlights of the Olympics* (Hastings, 1977)
Kieran, John and A. Daley. *The Story of the Olympic Games 776 B.C. to 1976* (Lippincott, 1977)
World Almanac: section on "Olympics"

MALE/FEMALE ROLES IN THE UNITED STATES

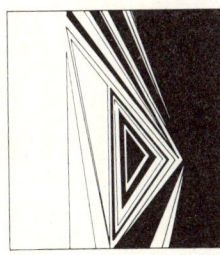 From the end of World War II until recent years, the lives of men and women in the United States usually had one form. Usually, men and women married. The man usually worked. He earned the money that the family needed. The woman took care of the children, cooked, and cleaned. In recent years, the role of men and women in the United States has begun to change. Some research has been done to study the changes that have occurred. Let us look at some of the ways in which these roles are changing.

In the traditional marriage, the man worked at a job to earn money for the family. Most men worked in an office, a factory, or some other place away from the home. Since the man earned the money, he paid the bills. The money was used for food, clothes, a house, and other family needs. The man made most of the decisions. He was the boss.

In the traditional marriage, the woman seldom worked away from the house. She stayed at home to care for the children and her husband. She cooked the meals, cleaned house, washed the clothes, and did other household work. Her job at home was very important.

In recent years, many couples continue to have a traditional relationship of this kind. The man has a job and earns the money for the family. The woman stays at home and cares for the children and the house. Many Americans are happy with this kind of marriage. But some other Americans have a different impression of marriage and family responsibilities.

The idea of marriage as a way of life has changed recently in the United States. First, not everyone tries to get married. Some people decide that they would rather live alone. Second, many people get married, and then find that they are not happy. Sometimes, these people end their marriages. They get a divorce to end the marriage. The number of divorces in the United States has increased in recent years. Marriage has changed in another way. Many people get married, but their marriages are very different from the traditional marriage relationships. The difference in the relationship is the result of different roles played by each spouse.

In recent years, the man has not always been the spouse who worked. Many men now stay at home part of the time. They help to take care of the children

Role Change

and the house. Since the man does not always earn all of the money (or any of it, in some cases), both the man and the woman may pay the bills. The man is not the most important person in the house. He may share many important decisions with the woman, and sometimes with the children. Sometimes the wife will decide, and sometimes the husband will decide. Or, all the family may decide together to go somewhere or do something. These are some of the ways that men's roles have changed.

In recent years, more and more women have been working. They may earn money to help their husbands. In some cases, they earn all of the money for the family. In this way, the woman and the man reverse their traditional roles. The woman earns all of the money, and the man stays at home to take care of the children and the house. More women recently have decided not to have children at all. Some women have children and continue to work. They do not leave their jobs just because they have children. These are some of the ways that women's roles have changed.

There are two important differences in male and female roles now. One is that both men and women have many more choices. They may choose to marry or to stay single. They may choose to work or stay at home. Both men and women may choose roles that are comfortable for them.

A second difference in male and female roles is that within marriage many decisions and responsibilities are shared. The husband and wife may choose to have children, or they may not. If they have children, the man may take care of them some of the time, all of the time, or not at all. The woman may want to stay at home and take care of the children. Or she may want to go to work. Men and women now decide these things together in a marriage. Many married people now share these decisions and the responsibilities of their families.

EXERCISES
Comprehension
1. Describe a traditional relationship between a man and a woman.
2. What parts of the relationship have changed?
3. Who was most important in a traditional marriage? Why?
4. Do any Americans still have a traditional marriage?
5. Explain three ways that marriage has changed in the United States.
6. Name some differences in men's roles.
7. Name some differences in women's roles.
8. How do men and women sometimes exchange their traditional roles?
9. Explain some of the choices that men and women have now.
10. List some of the responsibilities now shared by men and women in the United States.

Discussion
Part A
1. This essay gives some impressions of changes in the roles of males and females in America. How are impressions different from facts? How are impressions different from points of view?

2. What are the important parts of a traditional relationship? Do you enjoy this kind of relationship?
3. What do you think it would be like if you were married to an American? Would you ever marry an American? Why? Why not?
4. Give your view of the recent changes in male and female roles. Do you like the changes, or not? Why?
5. Compare male/female roles in America to male/female roles in your country.
    Part B
1. If you are a male, describe your relationship to females. If you are a female, describe your relationship to males.
2. Have your relationships changed recently? In what ways?
3. Are you married? If not, would you like to be married? Explain your point of view.

Directed Sentences

Directions: Make sentences using the following word groups. You may use any form of a given word. You may use the words in any order.

1. bills-factory
2. comfortable-role-relationships
3. cooked-married-traditional
4. divorce-occurred-society
5. form-impressions-spouse
6. institution-responsibilities-reverse
7. choice-marriage-somewhere
8. seldom-household

Culver

A traditional marriage

Suggested Reading
American magazines
Friedan, B. *The Feminine Mystique* (Norton, 1974)
Sheresky, N. and M. Mannes. *Uncoupling: The Art of Coming Apart* (Dell, 1973)

OPEN EDUCATION

An Opinion

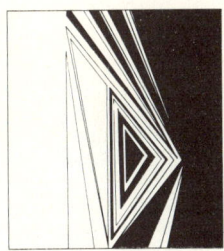 When people give their opinion about something, they give their feelings about the subject. In an opinion, a person says either that he or she likes an idea or thing, or she or he does not like it, and says why. This essay gives an opinion about open education. First, a definition of open education will be given. Then, some of the good things about open education and some of the bad things about open education will be described. And then, an opinion will be given. You may agree with the opinion, or not. You may agree with the opinion partly. You will have your own opinion.

This look at open education has two parts. The first part has to do with how the teacher feels about the students. The second part has to do with what the teacher does in the classroom. Each part of the definition can be explained by comparing open education with traditional education.

In traditional education, the teacher may feel that the students are not very grown up. Usually, teachers are older than students, and teachers feel that students are young and do not know very much about the world. The teachers feel that they must tell the students what to do most of the time, and that they must make the students study specific things. In open education, the teacher's feelings are very different. These teachers feel that the students are individuals first, and students second. They expect the students to be responsible for the things that they do, just as adults are. A student's ideas and feelings are just as important as the teacher's. The teacher allows the students to decide what they want to do, and does not make them study specific subjects or things. The teacher lets them decide what to study and how much to study. It is very important for the teacher to show how he or she feels about the students.

The second part of the idea of open education has to do with what the teacher does in the classroom. In the traditional classroom, the students are told what to do. There is a list of things that the students must do to finish the class. There are rules made by the teacher that the student must follow, even if the student sees no reason for the rules. In open education, the teacher allows the students to choose what to do. They may study, or talk, or do nothing at all if they want to. There are no specific things for the students to do. There are no traditional rules made by the teacher. The only rules in an open classroom are

An open classroom

rules for everyone's safety. The students are allowed to discover subjects in the open classroom, instead of being made to study them. Open education is a really complex idea.

There are some very good things about open education. This way of teaching allows the students to grow as people, and to develop their own interests in many subjects. Open education allows students to be responsible for their own education, as they are responsible for what they do in life. Some students do badly in a traditional classroom. The open classroom may allow them to enjoy learning. Some students will be happier in an open education school. They will not have to worry about grades or rules. For students who worry about these things a lot, it is a good idea to be in an open classroom.

But many students will not do well in an open classroom. For some students, there are too few rules. These students will do little in school. They will not make good use of open education. Because open education is so different from traditional education, these students may have a problem getting used to making so many choices. For many students it is important to have some rules in the classroom. They worry about the rules even when there are no rules. Even a few rules will help this kind of student. The last point about open education is that some traditional teachers do not like it. Many teachers do not believe in open education. Teachers who want to have an open classroom may have many problems at their schools.

You now know what open education is. Some of its good points and bad points have been explained. You may have your own opinion about open education. The writer thinks that open education is a good idea, but only in theory. In actual fact, it may not work very well in a real class or school. The writer believes that most students, but of course not all students, want some structure in their classes. They want and need to have rules. In some cases, they must be made to study some subjects. Many students are pleased to find subjects they have to study interesting. They would not study those subjects if they did not have to.

Some of the ideas of open education can be applied very easily. The teacher's feelings about the students can be changed in any kind of class. The teacher's feelings are important to the students. The teacher can apply some of the ideas of open education to a class easily. But changing the way the classroom is run is more difficult to do.

The writer thinks that some of the ideas of open education are very good, but that some are not good, and that it is hard to do some of the things open education suggests. Several ideas of open education as a different way of teaching students and a different way of running a class have been given. Some of the good and bad points about open education have been mentioned. The author has given one opinion about open education. What is your opinion?

EXERCISES
Comprehension
1. What is an opinion?
2. Define open education.

3. Explain two ways that open education is different from traditional education.
4. Why is open education a good idea?
5. What kinds of students do well in open education?
6. What kinds of students do badly in open education?
7. Name some other problems of open education.
8. What does the author think of open education? Why?
9. Why is it hard to apply the ideas of open education?
10. What ideas of open education may be easy to apply?

Discussion

Directions: In this essay, the writer is giving one point of view on a subject. In each opinion essay, the writer will give a point of view. It is important for you to know when a writer is giving his or her opinion on a subject. The questions for discussion following each opinion essay will help you to understand the writer's point of view (Part A) and to discover your own point of view on the subject (Part B).

Part A

1. Explain in your own words what an opinion is.
2. How do you know when a writer is giving an opinion?
3. Reread the essay. Where does the writer give an opinion?
4. Explain the writer's opinion of open education.

Part B

1. What is your opinion of open education?
2. Compare your opinion to the opinion of the writer.
3. Suppose that you are a teacher, and that you would like to use the ideas of open education. What would you do?
4. Describe some teachers you have had. Did you like them? Why or why not?

Andrew Botwick/Monkmeyer

A traditional classroom

Suggested Reading

Holt, John. *Freedom and Beyond* (Dutton, 1972)

Kohl, H. *The Open Classroom* (N.Y. Review of Books, 1969)

Neill, A. S. *Summerhill* (Hart, 1960)

Postman N. & C. Weingartner. *Teaching as a Subversive Activity* (Delacorte, 1969)

WORD STUDY REVIEW

To the student: These exercises will help you to learn new words in English more easily. Study each part carefully, and review new words from the first four chapters.

A. Noun ending: **-ion**

The ending *-ion* is added to words to make nouns meaning "the act of," "the state of," or "the result of." Usually "s" or "t" is put between the word and the ending. Add the ending *-ion* to the following words from the first four chapters:

compete-competit-_____   impress-impress-_____
contribute-contribut-_____   institute-institut-_____
decide-decis-_____   organize-organizat-_____
educate-educat-_____

B. Adjective ending: **-al**

The ending *-al* is added to words to make adjectives meaning "of," "like," or "suitable for." Add the ending *-al* to the following words from the first four chapters:

politics-politic-_____   tradition-tradition-_____
profession-profession-_____   vocation-vocation-_____

C. **Usage practice.**

Directions: Fill in the blank with the correct form of the word given in brackets [ ].

1. A university is one place for higher [educate] _____ in America.
2. There are many different [politics] _____ groups in the United States.
3. Doctors and lawyers are usually thought of as [profession] _____.
4. A [tradition] _____ person may have many problems in the modern world.
5. There is much [compete] _____ among young people to get good jobs.
6. Many people make large [contribute] _____ to charity groups.
7. Many young people must make a [decide] _____ whether to go to college or not.
8. [Vocation] _____ training helps many young people find good jobs.
9. [Institute] _____ such as colleges and universities allow many people to become well-educated.
10. Many people have very bad [impress] _____ of tourists.

TELEVISION

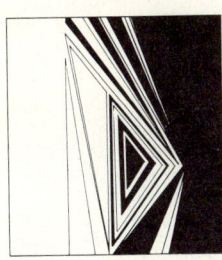

Most people in the United States watch TV, even though they complain about television sometimes. It's fun to watch TV, and it's easy. You turn on the TV, sit down in a comfortable chair, and see many different things. The people on TV will make you laugh and cry. They will inform you and excite you. By watching TV, you can hear the latest news from all over the world, and you can learn about new developments in science, art, literature, and technology. You can watch sports on TV. You can watch the Olympics, or a local sports event. Finally, in some places, it is possible to go to school by watching television. There are special classes on TV for high school and college students. A person may get a good education at home. These are some of the reasons for watching TV. There are other reasons.

There are many kinds of programs on TV. Many people like to watch special events on TV. Often, important political and social events can be watched on TV while they are happening. Many people, for example, watched the landing of the astronauts on the moon. A second kind of program that many people like to watch is called a talk show. On this kind of show, one person interviews several famous people. In the conversations, you can learn many interesting things about important people in theater, politics, sports, and other fields. A third kind of program that many people like to watch is a program in a foreign language. There are some TV channels which broadcast all of their programs in Spanish, French, or some other language. These programs are watched by many people who speak those languages. Students who are studying foreign languages sometimes watch these programs to learn the language better.

In spite of the fact that there are different kinds of programs, many people are concerned about television. One area they are concerned about is programming. This area has to do with what kinds of shows are on, and when they are on. One result of this concern was "Family Viewing Time." Many people did not like the fact that there were violent TV shows in the early evening. They felt that many children watched these programs, and as a result the children thought that violence is a good way to solve problems. It was agreed by the television industry that during Family Viewing Time (7–9 P.M.), no violent shows would be broadcast. Many people also feel that the programs are not always realistic. Too

Many people watching astronauts on TV

many programs do not show life as it really is. When all the shows in a series have a happy ending, people feel that this is very misleading. In real life, many things do not have a happy ending.

A second area of concern is advertising. Many people who watch a lot of TV complain that there is too much advertising. Most TV stations need to have advertisements to help pay for their expenses. The companies that advertise on TV pay for the time when their product is discussed, and this money is used by the TV station to pay for the programs we see. Many of the advertisements are shown over and over again. This can be both boring and annoying. The advertisers hope you will buy their products if you hear about them often enough. However, some people deliberately refuse to buy products that are advertised too much on TV.

Many parents in the United States are concerned about the effect of TV advertising on their children. Children may watch TV and may see candy advertised. The children may ask their parents to buy the candy they have seen on TV. The candy may not be good for the child's health. Also, children see many kinds of toys and games advertised on TV. If their parents cannot afford to buy these things, the children get upset. Many parents would like to have no advertising during the times when children watch TV—early evenings and weekends. Maybe some day all TV stations will stop advertisements. No one really likes them much, but they help to pay for the programs.

There are some TV stations that never have advertising. These are called noncommercial stations. There are two kinds of noncommercial stations: government sponsored stations and educational stations. When the government sponsors a station, the government pays for all of the station's expenses. In some countries this is the only kind of television there is. In England, for example, the British Broadcasting Company (BBC) is sponsored by the British government. This station has no advertising. An educational station is usually supported by some kind of educational institution such as a college or university. In the United States, most noncommercial TV stations are educational stations. An example of this kind of station is WKAR-TV, in Lansing, Michigan, which is sponsored by Michigan State University. This station also has no advertisements, and has many programs which are entertaining as well as educational.

Some of the complaints Americans have about TV have already been mentioned. There is too much advertising. There is too much violence. The third, and perhaps most important, complaint many people have about television is that the programs for adults are unsophisticated. Many adults feel that TV ought to be much better than it is.

In spite of all the complaints they have about TV programming and advertising, most people spend some of their time watching TV every day. Most people enjoy at least some of the things that they watch. They enjoy being entertained, and they enjoy being informed by programs on TV. Almost everyone likes sports programs, or special events, or news, or talk shows. Both commercial and noncommercial TV make important contributions to our lives.

EXERCISES
Comprehension
1. Why do people in the United States watch television?
2. What kinds of information can you get from TV?
3. List two other things you can see on TV.
4. Describe one type of program on American TV.
5. Discuss the American concern with programming.
6. Why do Americans complain about TV advertising?
7. What is a noncommercial TV station?
8. Explain the difference between government sponsored and educational TV stations.
9. What kinds of programs are on educational stations?
10. What is the most important complaint Americans have about TV?

Discussion
Directions: Answer questions in parts A and C if you are not in the United States. Answer questions in parts A, B, and C if you are in the United States.
Part A
1. Are the stations you watch commercial or noncommercial? Which do you like better?
2. Describe an important event you have seen on TV.
3. Is TV important to worldwide communication or not? Explain your opinion.
4. What do you think life was like before TV was invented? Was it good or bad?
5. Are people concerned about TV in your country? Discuss some of the important problems.

CBS/TV

Educational TV

Part B
1. Describe some American TV shows you like.
2. Describe some American TV shows you dislike.
3. What is your opinion of TV advertising?
4. Does watching TV in English help you to learn the language? In what ways?
5. In what ways can TV be made better? (Students may wish to write letters to a TV station as a result of this discussion.)
Part C
1. Do you watch TV? Why? Why not?
2. Have you ever seen yourself or a friend on TV? If so, explain what happened.
3. (Group exercise) Have all students watch one TV show. Evaluate the program as a class.

Directed Sentences

Directions: Make sentences using the following word groups. You may use any form of a given word. You may use the words in any order.

1. discussed-health
2. sponsored-solve
3. refuse-upset-companies
4. product-afford-possible
5. misleading-aspects-advertising
6. realistic-series
7. various-interviews-local
8. ought-noncommercial-deliberately
9. entertaining-cry-laugh
10. unsophisticated-boring-annoying
11. dislike-channels
12. conversations-learn-literature-technology
13. complaints-developments-educational
14. inform-feelings-politics
15. violent-industry

Suggested Reading

Black, Peter. *The Mirror in the Corner: People's Television* (Hutchinson, 1972)
Klavan, E. *Turn the Damned Thing Off* (Bobbs-Merrill, 1972)
Settel, I. *A Pictorial History of Television* (Grosset and Dunlap, 1969)

THE STOCK MARKET

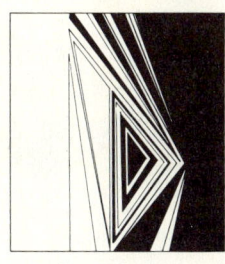

In the largest city in many countries around the world, you may want to visit the stock exchange. There are stock exchanges in Paris, London, Tokyo, Toronto, and many other places. One of the largest, most famous, and most important stock exchanges in the world is located in New York City. The market, as a stock exchange is sometimes called, is important to many people because they make money by investing in it. In this essay, the stock exchange itself will be explained, and the process of investing money in the stock market will be described.

Perhaps you can guess what happens at a stock market from its name. It is called a market because it is a place where some people sell things and others buy things. An exchange of things takes place. The things that are exchanged at the stock market are shares of stock in businesses or companies. The shares represent a partial ownership of the company. In other words, if you buy shares of stock in a business, you become a partial owner of the business. The stock market or stock exchange, then, is a place where people can buy or sell shares in a particular company or business.

Many different kinds of people buy shares of stock in the stock market. Some of these people are very wealthy. They have a lot of money; they have much more money than they really need for everyday living expenses. They buy shares of stock in hopes of getting more money than they have. Other people are not very rich, but they buy stock anyway. They may buy it to try to become rich. Or they may buy it as part of a plan to save money. There are many other reasons why people buy and sell stock. In general, everyone who buys or sells stock hopes to make money. All the people who buy stock are investing money in a company or business. They are called investors.

Why does a company want to share its money with other people? There are several reasons. First, the company may be doing very well. It may need money to expand. By selling shares of stock, the company can get the money it needs. Sometimes, it is advantageous for the company to "go public" for tax reasons. Because of the tax laws, the company may save money on taxes by selling shares on the stock exchange. Sometimes, a company may owe a lot of money to banks. By selling shares of stock, it may be able to pay the banks. Many companies sell

Edward C. Topple

The New York Stock Exchange

stock for this reason. However, the reasons why companies sell their stocks on the stock exchange are often complex. In general, all companies that sell shares of stock on the stock exchange need to raise money for one reason or another.

Investors who buy shares of stock in a company may make money in two ways. They may begin to make money right away. Suppose that a person invests in a company, and the company makes money. The company shares this money with the investor. This money that is shared is called a dividend. Dividends are usually sent to investors once every three months while they own the stock. A second way that investors may make money is to sell the stock at a higher price than they paid when they bought it. The price of each share of stock goes up if the company does very well. It may also go up for many other reasons. But when it does go up, a person may sell it and make a profit.

Here is an example of how this process works. Mr. and Mrs. Smith want to invest in the stock market. They have $1000 to invest. They talk to a person who can help them to buy a good stock. This person is called a stock broker. The broker is licensed to buy and sell stock on the stock market. The broker tells Mr. and Mrs. Smith about the Ward Pencil Company. This company is making a lot of money by manufacturing pencils. It is selling shares of stock in order to get money to expand. The shares cost $5.00 each. The Smiths decide to buy 100 shares of stock in the Ward Pencil Company. The broker fills this order, and the Smiths own these 100 shares. In three months, the Ward Pencil Company issues a dividend of $1.00 per share. The Smiths have 100 shares, so they get a $100 dividend. In one year, the company expands. The company sells many more pencils. The price of the stock goes up to $6.00 for each share. Mr. and Mrs. Smith decide to sell their stock in the Ward Pencil Company at $6.00 a share. They get back $600, plus all of the money they have received in dividends. This is a very good investment.

The process of investing money in the stock market is somewhat more complex than this. But for everyone who wants to invest money in the market, the process is basically the same. Almost all stock markets work the same way. In each country, of course, there are special laws for the stock market, to make sure that everyone has a fair chance to make money by investing.

Investing money in the stock market is not the safest way in the world to make more money. There is no guarantee, for example, that the Ward Pencil Company will do well, and that the stock will go up. The company may do badly. Then the stock will go down, and the investors will lose money. The stock may go up or down for a number of very complex reasons. Everyone wants the stock market to go up, but sometimes even when a company does well the stock may go down. This is usually true for all stocks.

Investing money in the stock market is a gamble. Everyone hopes to make money by investing. Companies that need money are glad that many people are willing to gamble in order to make money. The stock market is a very interesting and complex part of the business world.

EXERCISES

Comprehension

1. List three cities which have stock exchanges.
2. What happens at a stock exchange?
3. Who buys stock?
4. Why do people buy stock?
5. Why do companies sell stock?
6. Explain what dividends are.
7. What is a broker?
8. Explain why Mr. and Mrs. Smith's investment is a good one.
9. Why is investing money in the stock market a gamble?
10. Do all stocks always go up?

Discussion

Part A

1. Would you invest in the stock market? Why or why not?
2. Suppose you had $1000 to invest. What would you do with it? Why?
3. What are some other ways of investing money?
4. Suppose you own a company or business. Would you want the company to "go public"? Why? Why not?
5. Discuss some businesses you might like to invest in. Explain your choices.

Part B

1. Is there a stock market in your country? Where?
2. What are some different kinds of investments that you know about?
3. Have you ever visited a stock market? Describe it if you have.

Mahon/Monkmeyer

American Stock Exchange

Directed Sentences

Directions: Make sentences using the following word groups. You may use any form of a given word. You may use the words in any order.

1. plus-stock-profit
2. manufacturing-issues-dividend
3. somewhat-shares-advantageous
4. stock exchange-save-gamble-wealthy
5. sell-partial-licensed-broker
6. market-"go public"
7. true-basically-guarantee-price
8. in general-owe-bank
9. tax-raise-in hopes of
10. invest-order-ownership

Suggested Reading

Eiteman, W. J., et. al. *The Stock Market,* 4th ed. (McGraw-Hill, 1966)
Finley, H. *Everybody's Guide to the Stock Market* (Henry Regnery Co., 1968)
Financial pages of any major newspaper

WOMEN IN SPORTS

Women in the United States and in many other countries participate in a growing number of sports and games. This has not always been the case, however. In fact, women have not been as active in sports as men. Only in recent years have women begun to catch up to men in this area. Until the twentieth century, women did not often participate in sports.

Part of the explanation for this is that women simply did not have time. Many women cooked, cleaned, and took care of children. They were so busy that they did not have time for sports. A second reason, especially in the late nineteenth century, is that a woman's image at that time was one of frailty, illness, and delicacy. In the Victorian era, people thought that it was unladylike for a woman to be involved in any sports activity.

There have been changes in both the view of women in the modern world, and also changes within the world of sports. These changes have allowed many more women to participate in sports. The general view of women has changed substantially since the Victorian era. Women are no longer considered delicate. People do not think it is unladylike for a woman to compete in sports. Women who win in sports activities are highly regarded. Many women now take part in sports and games of many different kinds, and enjoy doing so. This development is partly the result of a change in the image of women in the modern world.

Women also are more active in sports now because of two changes in sports. First, in the early twentieth century, women began to compete regularly in the Olympics. Also, the number of events for women in the Olympics has been growing quite steadily. The fact that women can compete in the Olympics encourages many to become active in the various Olympic activities. In more recent years, television has had a noticeable effect on both the popularity of and participation in women's professional sports. Many women's competitions have been on TV, especially in the United States. Many women's tennis matches and golf matches are on TV, along with much other competition. Seeing women in professional sports on TV has made certain sports much more popular among women, as amateurs and as professionals.

Many American women are more active in sports now than ever before. This is the result of the developments in sports and in modern society. It is also

Evonne Goolagong

the result of the Women's Liberation Movement* in the United States. In particular, three groups of women are active in sports. Some women are sports professionals. These are women who participate in sports to earn money. Some women play in tennis matches or golf matches and if they win, they usually win a substantial amount of money. College women are a second group who are active in sports. Some of these women take a sport as part of their academic program. Tennis, golf, swimming, and other sports are available in college. They may take a course in gymnastics, or become a member of the women's track team. Some of these women compete against other women from other colleges, and some compete in national championships. If these collegiate women are very good, they may join the Olympic team, and compete in the Olympics. However, few women become professionals, and relatively few take a sport in college. Most women who are active in sports in the United States are amateurs. Women in this third group are those who play a game or sport because they like it. They may not be especially good at the sport, but they have fun playing it. Perhaps the largest number of women who have recently become active in sports are in this amateur group. Many of these women may have learned the sport in college, also. But the number of serious collegiate and professional women players is increasing steadily.

EXERCISES
Comprehension
1. Describe women's role in sports before the twentieth century.
2. What was the image of women in the Victorian era?
3. What is the image of women now?
4. How has this change in the image of women encouraged women in sports?
5. Describe the role of women in the Olympics.
6. Explain the effect of television on women's sports.
7. If a women is a professional athlete, what does she do?
8. Name some sports that college women are active in.
9. Describe women who are amateurs in sports.
10. There is very little information about women in sports. Why?

Discussion
   Part A
1. What do you think of women players? Why?
2. Do you think women are better at sports than men? Why or why not?
3. Do you think women should represent your country in international sports? Why or why not?
4. Discuss recent developments in women's sports in your country.
5. Do you think women should play in sports like soccer and baseball? Explain your point of view.

---

* See later chapter on Women's Liberation.

Part B

1. Are women active in sports in your country? If so, which sports do women play?
2. If you are a woman, are you active in sports?
3. Name some professional women athletes you know of. What sports do they play?

Directed Sentences

Directions: Make sentences using the following word groups. You may use any form of a given word. You may use the words in any order.

1. general-arenas-track
2. join-substantially
3. participate-golf-tennis-players
4. regarded-simply-growing
5. involved-noted
6. available-within-academic
7. significant-case-member
8. steadily-delicacy-illness-frailty-image
9. encourages-championships-national-noticeable
10. Victorian-considered-unladylike
11. collegiate-explanation-popularity-serious

Lawn Tennis

Suggested Reading

Gerber, Ellen, et. al. *The American Woman in Sport* (Addison-Wesley, 1974)
Harris, Dorothy ed. *Women and Sport* (Penn State, 1972)
Klafs, Carl & M. J. Lyon. *The Female Athlete* (C. V. Mosby Co., 1973)
Sports Illustrated

HISTORY
OF
BIOLOGY

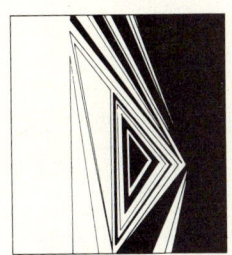
Contributions to the development of biology have come from all over the world. Three groups of biologists, working in the years since the Renaissance, will be studied here. Their contributions are important to the history of biology, and to modern science. The work of one man in each of the three groups will be studied.

The first group of biologists, and the earliest group to be studied here, are the microscopists of the 17th century. These people worked with microscopes. They built them and improved them for use in the study of science. Anthony van Leeuwenhoek, a Dutch microscopist who lived from 1632 until 1723, was one of the many important people in this group. Van Leeuwenhoek was interested in improving the lenses that were used in making microscopes. He made some microscopes, and looked at many different things with the help of the magnifying lenses which he made, also. By looking through the lenses, van Leeuwenhoek realized that there was a whole world filled with microscopic living things. Most people were unaware that these small living things existed. After van Leeuwenhoek and other microscopists made their work known, microscopes were improved, and many important discoveries in biology and medicine continued to be made. The microscope continues to be a very important tool in science today.

A second group of biologists worked in the 18th century to systematize our knowledge in science. They tried to organize all of the information found by many scientists so that everyone could use the same system for talking about discoveries. One system was developed by a Swedish scientist named Carl von Linnaeus, who lived from 1707 until 1778. He classified plants, animals, and minerals in a very useful way. His idea was to give each plant, animal, and mineral a two-part Latin name. The first part of the name was a general name. It told what general group of things the plant, animal, or mineral belonged to. This was the name of the *genus,* or group. The second part of the name was the specific name. This was the name of the *species,* or kind. It told what specific plant, animal, or mineral it was.

An example of Linnaeus' system is the Latin name for the flowers we call roses. All these flowers are in the general group or genus *Rosa.* Each kind of rose

The *Beagle*

has a specific name, which is the second word in the name. In Linnaeus' system, there are many species of the genus Rosa. Two examples are *Rosa damascena,* the damask rose, and *Rosa centifolia,* the hundred-fold or cabbage rose.

This system was extremely popular among scientists, and is still used today. There are several reasons for its popularity. First, the system is simple and clear. Second, Linnaeus used Latin words in his system and, at that time, nearly all scientists knew Latin. Everyone who knew Latin did not have to learn any special words. Also, the two names were a short description and were fairly easy to remember. Linnaeus's own books also explain the popularity of his system. His main area of interest was botany. Since he wrote the most complete botanical descriptions, his books were important references. In his botanical writings, each plant was given a two-part name using his system. Since his books were widely used, his system also became widely used. Linnaeus's system, which is still used today, is sometimes referred to as a system of binomial nomenclature. This term refers to the fact that Linnaeus gave two names to each thing.

A third group of biologists did most of their work in the 19th century. These scientists profited from the interest in world exploration during this time. They went on many expeditions as observers and collectors. Their job was to study the plants and animals of the new lands. One of the best-known explorers and observers was the great English biologist, Charles Darwin. He lived in England in the years from 1809 until 1882.

Since he was an explorer, Darwin did not spend all of the years of his life at home in England. He left England for five years in the early 1830's to travel on a ship called the *Beagle.* This trip is famous. For the other people on the *Beagle*, the purpose of the trip was to draw maps and to explore South America. They also planned to sail all the way around the earth. For Darwin, the purpose of the trip was different. He collected many samples of plants and animals from South America and the South Seas. He also wrote down many of his observations of the living things he found in his explorations. When he returned to England, Darwin wrote a book called *Origin of Species,* which was about evolution. His theory of evolution was developed as a result of his observations during his trip on the *Beagle.*

Van Leeuwenhoek, Linnaeus, and Darwin are three very important men in the history of biology. Each is one of a group of people who made a significant contribution to science. The contributions of all three can still be observed in modern science. If you study science, you will find microscopes in use in all kinds of scientific study. As part of your studies, you will probably have to learn the Latin names for all the animals and plants. The system developed by Linnaeus is still used in modern science. Darwin's theory of evolution is used by most scientists. It has helped modern biologists to understand the changes in plants and animals over many years. Evolution may help us understand some illnesses and help scientists keep people more healthy. These three men have made important contributions to science, but they are only a few of the important people in the history of biology.

EXERCISES

Comprehension

1. Who were the microscopists?
2. What did Van Leeuwenhoek do?
3. What is a microscope? Describe it.
4. Describe Linnaeus's system.
5. Why was the system popular?
6. What was Linnaeus's main area of interest?
7. What was the main group in 19th century biology?
8. Who was Darwin?
9. What was the *Beagle*? Why is it famous?
10. If you have studied science, explain the importance to modern science of microscopes, binomial nomenclature, or evolution.

Discussion

Part A

1. Is the information in this chapter helpful to you? Why or why not?
2. Have you worked with a microscope? Describe some things you have seen.
3. Biology and medicine are closely related subjects. Discuss the importance of each science in relation to the other.
4. Many developments in the history of biology are still important now. Describe any developments of this kind that you know about.

Part B

1. What sciences have you studied?
2. Do you like science? Why or why not?
3. Do you think it is important to know about biology? Explain your answer.

Bausch & Lomb

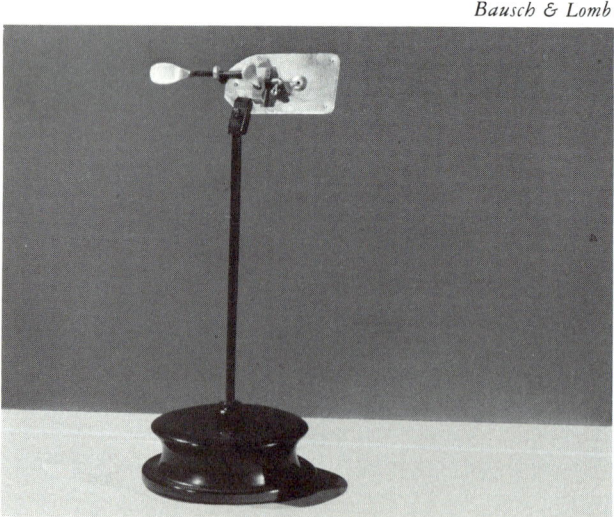

Van Leeuwenhoek's microscope

Directed Sentences

Directions: Make sentences using the following word groups. You may use any form of a given word. You may use the words in any order.

1. lenses-improved-microscopists
2. fairly-evolution-biology
3. systematize-botany-extremely
4. belonged-samples-collectors-classified
5. binomial nomenclature-reference-genus-species
6. Renaissance-magnifying-unaware
7. discoveries-explorer-observer

Suggested Reading

Darwin, Charles. *A Diary of the Voyage of H.M.S. Beagle* (Kraus Reprints, 1969)
Eiseley, Loren. *The Unexpected Universe* (Harcourt Brace Jovanovich, 1972)
de Kruif, Paul. *Microbe Hunters* (Harcourt Brace Jovanovich, 1966)
Lanham, Url. *Origins of Modern Biology* (Columbia University Press, 1968)
Watson & Crick. *The Double Helix* (New American Library, 1969)

COOPERATIVE EFFORTS IN THE WORLD AROUND US

An Opinion

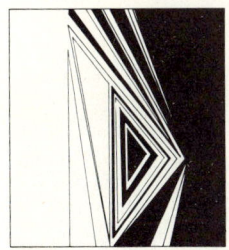 In this world around us, there are two things that do not belong to any one country. One of these things is the large amount of water on the earth. A certain amount of the ocean surrounding each country is considered to belong to that country, but much of the ocean is not owned by anyone. The air is also not owned by any country. In both the air and the water, there is much pollution. No one can agree on what to do about the pollution. People are concerned about the air and the water used by everyone, and they are also concerned about the future of the earth. Some of the problems of water and air pollution follow. One possible way of solving the pollution problem will be given.

One of the most important pollution problems is in the oceans. Outside each country's part of the ocean, there is a large amount of water. Many ships sail in this water. Some ships are fishing ships. Some ships carry oil. Some ships carry people across the oceans. All of these ships are affected by the pollution problem. The fishing ships may have to travel a long distance to find fish. Fish must have clean water to live in. If the water is dirty, the fish will move to another part of the ocean. This makes fishing difficult. The oil ships sometimes lose some of their oil in the water. This may kill the fish and other animals. It certainly makes the ocean dirty. Someone must clean up the pollution from the oil ships. Ships that carry people also carry the trash that people make. If the trash is put in the ocean, it too can make the water dirty. Someone must clean up this pollution also. It is not a pleasure for people to travel in dirty water in the ocean. The problem is that our oceans are becoming more and more dirty and no one cleans them up.

A second important pollution problem is in the air. In many places, the air is dirty. This is especially true in big cities. In big cities, there are many cars, and usually many large airplanes. Also, there may be large factories. Cars, airplanes, and factories make air pollution in many complex ways. This air does not belong to anyone, but everyone must use it. It is not good for us to have dirty air. Someone must clean up the air, but no one is doing it.

A third important pollution problem is not really on the earth. It is in the air around the earth. We do not use all of this air. Part of the air that is very high

Thin ozone layer

up from the earth's surface screens the earth from the sun. It is a special kind of air called ozone. It gives the whole earth protection from the very strong light of the sun. Different kinds of air pollution have been destroying this very high air. The air pollution from cars and factories has been destroying this ozone. The ozone gives us less protection from the sun because of the pollution. It is becoming less helpful in keeping the dangerous light of the sun away from the earth. This is not healthy for us. In a short time it may be dangerous to walk outside on a sunny day. Someone must clean the upper air around the earth, but no one takes responsibility for it, either.

There is a lot of pollution in the air and in the water. It is very dangerous. It is a difficult problem. Right now, no one is really trying to solve the pollution problem. The writer thinks that someone must try to solve this problem. Some countries are trying to solve their own pollution problems, inside their own limits. But most countries are not trying to clean up the pollution in the air and the water that belongs to everyone. Something must be done soon about the dirty air and water that are shared by everyone.

The writer thinks that we should have an International Earth Committee to work on pollution problems. It could do three things. First, it could make laws. These laws would take care of the air and the water that do not belong to any country. Second, the scientists on the committee could tell all countries what things make pollution. The scientists could try to find other ways for people to do the same things without making pollution. Third, the committee could do experiments. They could study the pollution in the world, and try to find ways to clean it up. An International Earth Committee could help us solve many of the problems of pollution. It is one possible way to solve the international pollution problem. Perhaps you can think of some other ways.

Would an International Earth Committee really help? It is hard to be sure. The writer thinks it may help. Pollution is a very important international problem. Everyone is going to have to help to solve this problem. You will probably be here on earth for many years. Your children and grandchildren will live here even longer. In a few years, no one may be able to go outside at all. Someone must begin to work on the problems of air and water pollution all around the earth. Everyone, in all of the countries on earth, must help to clean up the air and the water.

What do you think?

EXERCISES
Comprehension
1. What two things in the world do not belong to any country?
2. Does any part of the ocean belong to a particular country?
3. Describe the pollution problem in the ocean.
4. Does anyone take care of pollution in the oceans?
5. Why is the air we use so dirty?
6. Why is pollution of the upper air so dangerous?
7. What may happen if the upper air is not cleaned up?

8. Describe the International Earth Committee.
9. How could the Committee help to solve pollution problems?
10. What does the writer think may happen if the pollution problem is not solved?

Discussion

Part A
1. What is the writer's opinion about pollution?
2. How does the writer think the pollution problem can be solved?
3. Is this the only way to solve this problem?

Part B
1. Do you agree with the writer's view on pollution? Why or why not?
2. Describe some kind of pollution that affects you.
3. Is your country working on pollution?
4. Do you think international work on pollution will help world understanding and peace? Explain your point of view.

Suggested Reading

Borgese, Elizabeth. *The Drama of the Oceans* (Harry N. Abrams, 1976)
Brubaker, Sterling. *To Live On Earth* (Johns Hopkins, 1972)
Carson, Rachel. *Silent Spring* (Fawcett World, 1973)
Collier, Boyd. *Dynamic Ecology* (Prentice-Hall, 1973)
Falk, Richard. *This Endangered Planet* (Random House, 1971)

George Hall/Woodfin Camp

Cleaning up after oil spill

WORD STUDY REVIEW

To the student: These exercises will help you to learn new words in English more easily. Study each part carefully, and review new words from the first nine chapters.

A. Noun Ending: **-ion**
   Here are some more words like those you studied in Chapter 5, which use the noun ending *-ion.* Add the ending *-ion* to these words:
   converse-conversat_____   observe-observat_____
   evolve-evolut_____   participate-participat_____
   explain-explanat_____

B. Adjective ending: **-al**
   Here are some more words like those you studied in Chapter 5, which use the adjective ending *-al.* Add the ending *-al* to these words:
   botany-botanic_____
   education-education_____
   nation-nation_____

C. Negative prefixes: **non-, dis-** and **un-**
   The beginnings *non-, dis-* and *un-* are added to words to make their meanings negative. Add the correct negative form to each of the following words from the first nine chapters:
   not like_____   not aware_____
   not academic_____   not ladylike_____
   not commercial_____   not sophisticated_____

D. Noun endings: **-er** and **-or**
   The endings *-er* and *-or* are added to words to make nouns meaning a person or thing having to do with. Add the endings *-er* and *-or* to the following words from the first nine chapters:
   explore-explor_____   observe-observ_____
   invest-invest_____   profess-profess_____

E. **Usage practice**
   Directions: Fill in the blank with the correct form of the word given in brackets [   ].
   1. [Invest] _____ may make a lot of money in the stock market.
   2. Most people are [not aware] _____ of the problem of pollution.
   3. Noam Chomsky is a linguistics [profess] _____ at M.I.T.
   4. Darwin made many [observe] _____ while sailing on the *Beagle*.
   5. Some television programs may be very [education] _____.
   6. There are several [explain] _____ for the popularity of sports.
   7. People who are interested in plants often go to a [botany] _____ garden.
   8. Some people [not like] _____ all sports and games.
   9. If two people talk to each other, they may be having a [converse] _____ or a fight.

THE NOBEL PRIZE

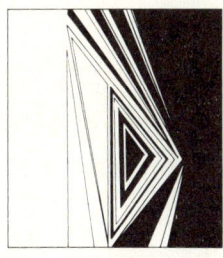 A Nobel Prize is one of the most highly regarded international honors a person can receive. These prizes were named for Alfred Nobel, a Swedish chemist and inventor. The first Nobel Prizes were awarded in 1901, five years after Nobel's death. Many famous people from all over the world have been awarded Nobel Prizes for their achievements. There are five different prizes: three in various sciences, one for literature, and the Peace Prize. But how did the prizes start?

Alfred Nobel was a chemist. He invented dynamite, and developed detonators for dynamite and for other explosives. As a result of these two inventions, he became a very wealthy man. He used part of his money to invest in oil. He made good investments and became even more wealthy. However, in spite of his great wealth, Nobel was not a happy man. He never married or had children. Also, he was a sick man a large part of his life. Nobel died at the age of sixty-three in 1896. He left all of his money in a trust fund. This money is held by a group of people who run the Nobel Foundation. The Nobel Foundation holds Nobel's money and gives the prizes.

The prizes are awarded by the Nobel Foundation for outstanding achievements or contributions in five areas. A prize is given in chemistry, physics, medicine or physiology, literature, and peace. Each prize has three parts. The first part is a gold medal. Second, a winner of a Nobel Prize is given a diploma saying that he has been awarded the prize. The third part of the prize is a large amount of money.

Often a prize is awarded to just one person, but not always. Sometimes a prize is shared. It may be awarded to two or more people who have worked together to reach a goal. Since the Nobel Prizes are international prizes, scientists, inventors, writers, and diplomats from all countries may receive a prize. Sometimes, two people from countries with different political views may even share a prize. An example of this is the 1973 Peace Prize, which was awarded to Henry Kissinger of the United States and to Le Duc Tho of North Vietnam for the Vietnam peace negotiations. It is also sometimes true that a prize is not given. If there is no outstanding achievement in one of the five areas, no prize is given in that area. In 1972, for example, no Nobel Peace Prize was given.

Dr. Rosalyn Yalow (1977 Nobel Prize in Medicine) and King Carl of Sweden

Someone must decide whether or not to give an award. The process of nominating and choosing Nobel Prize winners has two parts. First, nominations, or recommendations of people who might deserve a Nobel Prize, are made. The nominations in physics and chemistry are made by the Royal Academy of Science in Stockholm. The nominations in medicine or physiology are made by the Caroline Medical Institute, which is also in Stockholm. The Swedish Academy, along with the French and Spanish Academies, makes nominations in literature. The peace prize nominations are made by a committee of the Norwegian government. Many nominations are made in each area. Nominations from these groups begin the process of choosing the Nobel Prize winners.

The second part of the process of choosing Nobel prize winners is to decide which of the nominees deserves the award in each area. This decision is made by the Nobel Foundation in Stockholm. The Foundation may decide to give the awards to an individual or to several people in each area. Or the Foundation may decide not to give a prize at all in any area.

You probably know the names of some of the recent winners of the Nobel Prizes. The two winners who shared the 1973 Peace Prize, Henry Kissinger and Le Duc Tho, have already been mentioned. Because most of the prizes have been awarded in most years since 1901, there have been many winners. Some other recent winners of the Peace Prize are Willy Brandt of the Federal Republic of Germany in 1971, Dag Hammerskjöld of Sweden in 1961, and Albert Schweitzer of France in 1952. In other words, the Peace Prize was awarded to individuals in 1971, 1961, and 1952. In 1973, the Peace Prize was shared, and so was the prize in medicine or physiology. In that year, three people shared the prize in medicine or physiology. Two Austrians, Karl von Frisch and Konrad Lorenz, and an Englishman named Nikolass Tinbergen shared the prize. In 1962, also, the same prize had been shared by three men: two Englishmen, Francis Crick and Maurice Wilkins, and an American, James Watson. In literature, most of the prizes have been awarded to an individual each year. Pablo Neruda, a Chilean poet, won the prize for literature in 1971. Alexsander Solzhenitsyn of the USSR, Jean Paul Sartre of France, and Saul Bellow of the United States have also been awarded this prize recently.

In the 20th century, a Nobel Prize has been awarded to many people from countries all over the world. The winners of Nobel Prizes are honored for their great achievements and are rewarded both by prestige and by money for their contributions to human life. A Nobel Prize is one of the highest honors any scientist, diplomat, or writer can ever receive.

EXERCISES
Comprehension
1. Who was Alfred Nobel?
2. Describe the Nobel Prizes.
3. List the five areas in which prizes are awarded.
4. Is a Nobel Prize always given to individuals?
5. In what way is the Nobel Prize international?

6. How are nominations made?
7. Who chooses the winners?
8. Is there always a winner?
9. Name some of the recent winners.
10. How are the winners rewarded?

Discussion
Part A
1. Name some Nobel Prize winners you know.
2. For some of the winners you know, or for those listed in this essay, explain why the award was given.
3. Does your country give prizes for outstanding achievement in any area? Describe these prizes.
4. Name some famous people who you feel should receive a Nobel Prize.
Part B
1. Have you ever received a prize or honor? Explain.
2. Some people have refused a Nobel Prize. Why would a person do this? Can you think of any recent examples?
3. Do you think the Nobel Peace Prize contributes to world peace? If so, how? If not, why not?
4. Do you think the Nobel Prizes are a good idea? Explain your point of view.
5. A Nobel Prize winner now receives over $100,000 as part of the prize. How do you think this affects the award?

United Press International

The Nobel Peace Medal

Directed Sentences

Directions: Make sentences using the following word groups. You may use any form of a given word. You may use the words in any order.

1. poet-outstanding-medal
2. diplomats-negotiations-peace
3. invent-dynamite
4. invention-detonators-explosives
5. winner-reward-trust fund
6. great-nominee-background
7. whether-deserve-nomination
8. prestige-honor-prize-nominate
9. recommendation-Royal Academy of Science-Caroline Medical Institute-award
10. academy-chemist-inventor
11. chemistry-physics-physiology

Suggested Reading

Evlanoff, Michael. *Alfred Nobel, The Loneliest Millionaire* (W. Ritchie Press, 1969)
Nobel Foundation, ed. *Nobel, The Man and His Prizes* (American Elsevier, 1972)
World Almanac section on Nobel Prize winners

ize 65

ANIMAL LANGUAGE

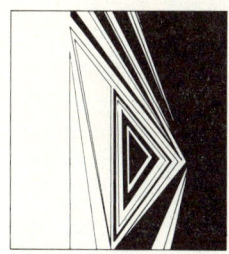 Some people say that human beings are the only animals that have language. Is this true? It is a very difficult question to anwer. A person must have a good definition of "language." Different kinds of animals must be studied. Some animals certainly seem to have a communication system. That system may or may not be a language. For example, the bee has ways of telling other bees about food. The dolphin, a kind of fish, has ways of giving information to other dolphins. The monkey, an animal that is similar to humans in many ways, can use a human language system. Does this mean animals have language? We will study each of these animals to try to answer this question.

Bees are very small animals which fly through the air to look for flowers for food. Bees have been studied by Karl von Frisch who won a Nobel Prize for his work. He studied bees' activities when they returned to their home called a hive. When a bee found some food, it returned to the hive and danced. The dance was the way the bee communicated to other bees the fact that it had found food.

Bees do two kinds of dances to tell other bees of their discovery of food. First, there is a round dance. In this dance, the bee moves in a circle inside the hive. The round dance is used when food is close by. The food must not be more than ten meters away. If a bee comes back and does a round dance, other bees know they must go out and look nearby for food. The bees also smell the bee that has found the food. The smell tells them what kind of flower to look for. After watching the round dance and smelling the bee that has found the food, the other bees can find the food source.

A second kind of dance done by the bees is a tail-wagging dance. In this dance, the bee wiggles the end of its body as it moves in a straight line. The tail-wagging dance is used when the food is far away. The food must be more than ten meters away. The bees know from the speed of the tail-wagging dance just how far away the food source is. The line the bee dances on shows the direction that the bees must fly in to find the food. In the tail-wagging dance, the bees also smell the bee that has found the food. The smell tells them what kind of flower to look for. After watching the tail-wagging dance and smelling the bee that has found the food, the other bees know three things. They know how far to fly, what direction to fly in, and what kinds of flowers to look for.

Lana

The bees' communication system is extremely interesting. Each bee can tell all the other bees where to look for food. The bees can also tell one another if the food is especially good, and how much of it there is. Karl von Frisch did an experiment with bees. He put a food source very high above the bee hive, and put a bee into the food. The bee returned to the hive and did the round dance, but none of the other bees could find the food. This suggests that bees do not really have a language. One bee could not tell the other bees the height of the food. One bee could not communicate this new information to the others.

Dolphins, like bees, have been studied to see if they have a language. Although scientists have not studied the dolphin as carefully as they have studied the bee, they have made interesting discoveries. Many observations have been made. A few experiments with dolphins have been done. The dolphin has been studied because its general behavior is much like that of humans. For communication, however, the dolphin's system is much more limited than a person's. The dolphin has three kinds of calls or noises to tell other dolphins about food, danger, or other things.

It seems that bees and dolphins communicate, but that they do not have language. It is much more difficult to decide whether monkeys have language. Monkeys are very intelligent and similar to humans. Because of this similarity, some scientists in the late 1940's tried to teach a monkey named Viki to talk. After a year, Viki could only say a few words. Part of the problem with this experiment is that monkeys do not have the same kind of mouth and throat as humans. They are not really able to make human speech sounds. As a result, the experiment with Viki did not work well.

In the mid-1960's, other scientists tried to teach a monkey named Washoe to use a sign language. In a sign language, words are not spoken. Instead, signs are made with the hands. Many people who cannot speak or hear use this sign language. It seemed to be a better kind of language to teach to a monkey. After two years, Washoe could make thirty-four signs with her hands. For example, she could put three fingers next to her ear as a sign for her name, Washoe. She could also use the sign for "come here," putting her arm out, and bending it back toward herself. She could also do two other things. First, she combined signs to make sentences. Second, she used one sign for all things of one kind, generalizing her use of the sign. The ability to combine and to generalize is important in language use.

A third group of scientists have been working with a monkey named Lana in the past few years. Lana is being studied at the Yerkes Primate Research Center in the United States. The scientists who are working with Lana are studying her ability to make sentences. She makes sentences by pressing symbols on a computer board. Lana may ask the computer to give her food, water, or toys. She must press the symbols in a correct sentence order to get what she wants. Lana has learned to use the nearly 100 symbols on the computer board. She can also use the symbols on the computer to answer simple questions which the scientist asks, using the computer also. She has shown that she understands sentences in two ways. First, she can correct the word order in a sentence. If the scientist presses the symbols in the wrong order, Lana will press them correctly. Lana has also shown that different word orders have different meanings for her. Lana's achievements are quite amazing. Does she have a language?

Of course, the answer to this question depends on how "language" is defined. We may define language as any system for exchanging information. If this definition is used, then bees, dolphins, and monkeys all have a language. But language may be defined in another way. We may define language as a system for exchanging information by making new combinations of symbols. If this definition is used, then bees and dolphins do not have a language, but monkeys may have one. Monkeys are clearly able to combine symbols in a human language that they have been taught. This is not their usual language, however.

Animal language, then, is a very complex thing. Many experiments are being done now to decide whether animals have a language. These experiments are interesting because they tell us more about animals. They are also interesting because they may help us learn language. The system used to teach Washoe has helped some humans to learn language. These experiments are a help to humans. We really cannot say whether animals have language or not. Much more research will have to be done before we can be sure.

EXERCISES
Comprehension
1. Describe the bees' communication system in general.
2. Explain the difference between the bees' round dance and their tail-wagging dance.
3. How are the two dances similar?
4. Describe von Frisch's experiment with the bees.
5. Why have dolphins been studied by scientists?
6. Why was the experiment with the monkey named Viki a failure?
7. What special abilities did Washoe have?
8. Describe the work that has been done with Lana.
9. Give two definitions of language.
10. Have humans been helped by animal language experiments? How?

Discussion
Part A
1. Define language in your own words.
2. Do you think animals have language? Why or why not?
3. Do you know of other animals whose communication systems have been studied by people?
4. What other animals should scientists study? Why?
Part B
1. Discuss the good points about the research described here.
2. Discuss the bad points about the research described here.

3. How do you feel about using animals for scientific research? Explain your view.
4. Are human and animal language really different? Give specific reasons for your answer.

Bees communicating

Directed Sentences

Directions: Make sentences using the following word groups. You may use any form of a given word. You may use the words in any order.

1. Yerkes Primate Research Center-computer-symbols-combinations
2. tail-wagging-wiggle-speed-smell
3. bee-hive-circle
4. monkey-throat-speech-intelligent
5. dolphin-behavior-amaze-similarity
6. definition-generalize-combine
7. communicate-correct

Suggested Reading

von Frisch, Karl. *The Dance Language and Orientation of Bees* (Harvard University Press, 1969)
Hayes, Catherine. *The Ape in Our House* (Harper & Row, 1951)
Lenneberg, Eric. *The Biological Foundations of Language* (Wiley, 1967)
Science magazine

NEWS
SOURCES

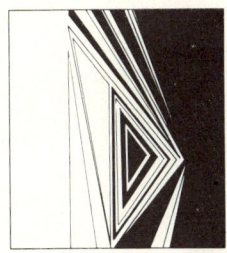

In the United States and in many other countries around the world, there are four main ways for people to be informed about developments in the news: newspapers, magazines, and radio or television news broadcasts. A person may use one, or all, of these sources for information. Each source is useful in its own way. Newspapers and magazines can give much information about a particular event. They may provide some history of the event, some of its causes, some of its effects, or perhaps give an opinion or point of view on a particular development. Radio and television can help a person to be well-informed about what is happening each day. It is also possible to listen to the radio or watch TV and do something else at the same time. Many people can listen to the news on their car radio while driving somewhere. For the student of English as a foreign language, an English language newspaper may be the most helpful news source that will also give you practice in reading English.

Most daily English language newspapers are not very hard to read. They are interesting and helpful in many ways. In some of them, you may be able to find news about your native country. You will find news and information about important national and international political developments. No matter what you are interested in, you can probably find something in the newspaper about it. A story in the newspaper may help you solve a problem. Other stories may be about good movies, concerts, or TV shows.

Usually, an English language newspaper has several sections or parts. Each part of the newspaper contains stories about different kinds of news. Some sections have a lot of advertisements which may be helpful if you want to save money. By reading the advertisements, you may find something you want on sale. Or you may find that two stores are advertising the same thing, but at one store the price is lower. Other sections may have fewer advertisements or have only a specific type of advertisement to interest the people who read that section of the paper.

The first section of the paper usually has the most important news in it. Important developments in national and international government and politics will be mentioned in the first section, and usually on the first page. Other news

"All the News
That's Fit to Print"

The New York Times

VOL. CXVIII....No. 40,721   NEW YORK, MONDAY, JULY 21, 1969   10 CENTS

LATE CITY EDITION

Weather: Rain, warm today; clear tonight. Sunny, pleasant tomorrow. Temp. range: today 80-66; Sunday 71-66. Temp.-Hum. Index yesterday 69. Complete U.S. report on P. 30.

MEN WALK ON MOON

ASTRONAUTS LAND ON A PLAIN AFTER STEERING PAST CRATER

Voice From Moon: 'Eagle Has Landed'

EAGLE (the lunar module): Houston, Tranquility Base here. The Eagle has landed.

HOUSTON: Roger. Tranquility, we copy you on the ground. You've got a bunch of guys about to turn blue. We're breathing again. Thanks a lot.

TRANQUILITY BASE: Thank you.

HOUSTON: You're looking good here.

TRANQUILITY BASE: A very smooth touchdown.

HOUSTON: Eagle, you are stay for T1. [The first step in the lunar operation.] Over.

TRANQUILITY BASE: Roger. Stay for T1.

HOUSTON: Roger and we see you venting the ox.

TRANQUILITY BASE: Roger.

COLUMBIA: How do you read me?

HOUSTON: Columbia, he has landed Tranquility Base. Eagle is at Tranquility. I read you five by. Over.

COLUMBIA (the command and service module): Yes, I heard the whole thing.

HOUSTON: Well, it's a good show.

COLUMBIA: Fantastic.

TRANQUILITY BASE: I'll second that.

APOLLO CONTROL: The next major stay-no stay will be for the T2 event. That is at 21 minutes 26 seconds after initiation of power descent.

COLUMBIA: Up telemetry command reset to reacquire on high gain.

HOUSTON: Copy. Out.

APOLLO CONTROL: We have an unofficial time for that touchdown of 102 hours, 45 minutes, 42 seconds and we will update that.

HOUSTON: Eagle, you loaded R2 wrong. We want 10254.

TRANQUILITY BASE: Roger. Do you want the horizontal 55 15.2?

HOUSTON: That's affirmative.

APOLLO CONTROL: We're now less than four minutes from our next stay-no stay. It will be for one complete revolution of the command module.

One of the first things that Armstrong and Aldrin will do after getting their next stay-no stay will be to remove their helmets and gloves.

HOUSTON: Eagle, you are stay for T2. Over.

Continued on Page 4, Col. 1

VOYAGE TO THE MOON

By ARCHIBALD MacLEISH

Presence among us,
    wanderer in our skies,
dazzle of silver in our leaves and on our
    waters silver,

    O
silver evasion in our farthest thought—
"the visiting moon" . . . "the glimpses of the moon" . . .
and we have touched you!

    From the first of time,
before the first of time, before the
first men tasted time, we thought of you.
You were a wonder to us, unattainable,
a longing past the reach of longing,
a light beyond our light, our lives—perhaps
a meaning to us . . .

    Now
our hands have touched you in your depth of night.

Three days and three nights we journeyed,
steered by farthest stars, climbed outward,
crossed the invisible tide-rip where the floating dust
falls one way or the other in the void between,
followed that other down, encountered
cold, faced death—unfathomable emptiness . . .

Then, the fourth day evening, we descended,
made fast, set foot at dawn upon your beaches,
sifted between our fingers your cold sand.

We stand here in the dusk, the cold, the silence . . .

and here, as at the first of time, we lift our heads.
Over us, more beautiful than the moon, a
moon, a wonder to us, unattainable,
a longing past the reach of longing,
a light beyond our light, our lives—perhaps
a meaning to us . . .

    O, a meaning!

over us on these silent beaches the bright
earth,
    presence among us

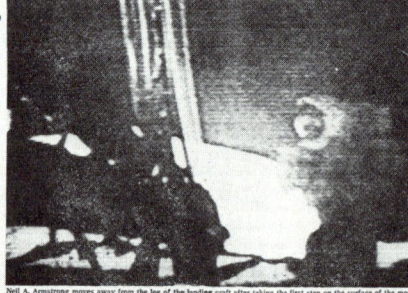

Neil A. Armstrong moves away from the leg of the landing craft after taking the first step on the surface of the moon.

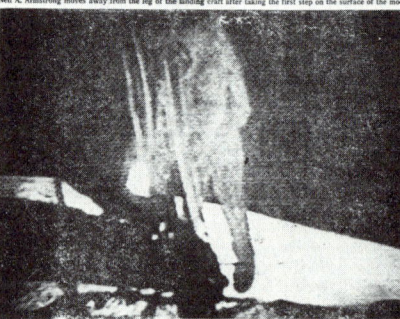

Col. Edwin E. Aldrin Jr., climbing down the ladder. The television camera was attached to a side of the lunar module.

Mr. Armstrong, right, rejoins Colonel Aldrin after placing the camera on a tripod about 60 feet away from the craft.

A Powdery Surface Found by Armstrong

By JOHN NOBLE WILFORD
Special to The New York Times

HOUSTON, Monday, July 21—Men have landed and walked on the moon.

Two Americans, astronauts of Apollo 11, steered their fragile, four-legged lunar module safely and smoothly to the historic landing at 4:17:40 P.M., Eastern daylight time, yesterday.

Neil A. Armstrong, the 38-year-old civilian commander, radioed to the earth and the control room here:

"Houston, Tranquility Base here. The Eagle has landed."

The first men to reach the moon—Mr. Armstrong and his co-pilot, Col. Edwin E. Aldrin Jr. of the Air Force—brought their craft to rest on a level, rock-strewn plain near the southwestern shore of the arid Sea of Tranquility.

About 6½ hours later, at 10:56:20 P.M., Mr. Armstrong opened the landing craft's hatch, stepped slowly down the ladder and planted the first human footprints on the lunar crust as millions around the world watched on television.

'Giant Leap for Mankind'

"That's one small step for man, one giant leap for mankind." Mr. Armstrong said as he stepped on the moon.

His first steps were tentative.

Testing to see how firm was the lunar soil.

"The surface appears to be very, very fine grained." Mr. Armstrong radioed. "It's almost sort of a powder—down there, it's very fine."

He quickly discovered he had no difficulty moving around in his bulky spacesuit and in the gravity that is one-sixth that of earth. He called it "very comfortable." His footprints, he said, were shallow. The rocket blast on landing had dug out a crater only a foot deep, he reported.

Colonel Aldrin joined him on the surface at 11:16 P.M. to start their rock-gathering and exploration.

Outside their vehicle the astronauts found a bleak world. It was just after dawn, with the sun low over the eastern horizon behind them and the chill of the long lunar night still clinging to the boulders, small craters and hills before them.

Colonel Aldrin said that one could see "literally thousands of small craters" and a low hill out in the distance.

But most of all he was impressed initially by the variety of shapes, angularities, granularities of the rocks and soil where the landing craft, code-named Eagle, had set down.

The landing came about four miles west of the aiming point, but well within the designated area. An apparent error in some data fed into the craft's guidance computer from the ground was said to have accounted for the discrepancy.

Suddenly the astronauts were startled to see that the computer was guiding them toward a possibly disastrous touchdown in a boulder-filled crater about the size of a football field.

Mr. Armstrong grabbed manual control of the vehicle and guided it safely over the crater to a smoother spot, the final seconds of descent.

Dramatic Triumph for Man

Soon after the landing, upon checking and finding the spacecraft in good condition, Mr. Armstrong and Colonel Aldrin made their decision to open the hatch and get out more than five hours earlier than originally scheduled.

"Our recommendation at this point is planning EVA (Extra Vehicular Activity) with your concurrence starting at 8 o'clock this evening, Houston time [9 P.M., E.D.T.], about three hours from now," Mr. Armstrong radioed ground control.

"Tranquility Base. Houston. We've thought about it. We will support it," ground control replied.

It was man's first landing on another world, the realization of centuries of dreams, the fulfillment of a decade of striving, a triumph of modern technology and personal courage, the most dramatic demonstration of what man can do if he applies his mind and measures with single-minded determination.

The moon, long the symbol of the impossible and the inaccessible, was now within man's reach, the first port of

Continued on Page 3, Col. 1

Today's 4-Part Issue of The Times

This morning's issue of The New York Times is divided into four parts. The first part is devoted to news of Apollo 11 and includes Editorials and letters to the Editor (Page 26). Poems on the landing on the moon appear on Page 17.

General news begins on the first page of the second part. The News Summary and Index is on the first page of the third part, which includes sports news, obituaries (Page 51) and transportation news and weather reports (Pages 50 and 52).

NEWS INDEX

that is important to the people who read the paper will also be in the first section. For example, *The New York Times* usually has stories about national and international news on the first page. There and on the other pages of the first section, the *Times* also has news about New York City and other nearby areas. This local news is important to many people who read *The New York Times.*

Many daily English language newspapers have several other sections. These sections are folded separately. This way, if two people want to read the paper, one person may read the news in the first section while another person reads a different section. Sports news is often printed in this way, in a separate part of the paper. Many people are interested in the sports news. In the United States, a newspaper will usually print stories about the important teams in the area. They may print stories about whether the team won or lost, and perhaps a complete report of a game or event. Much other sports news is included. Usually, scores are given from other games played by other teams around the country. Sometimes international sports news is given too. Reports on the Olympics while they are in progress are often given. Other major sports events in other countries may be reported too. World Cup soccer scores and Davis Cup tennis scores are given when these matches are played. Because many people have an interest in sports, sports news is almost always included in the daily newspaper.

Many English language newspapers carry a section of "features." Features are not really news stories but they are often informative and helpful. A feature story may tell you how to lose weight, save money, fix your car, or other helpful things. Features may also be about people in the community or local area. These local people may be important members of the community. They may be leaders of groups in the community, or they may be people who can help others in some way. It is often interesting to read about these people. Some features may be about important people in the news. *The New York Times* has a regular feature called "Man in the News" or "Woman in the News" in which much information is given about a particularly important person in the news of the day. Sometimes the person is an American. Other times the person may be an international political leader or even a person in sports or show business.

Another section which is found in most English language newspapers is called the opinion or editorial section. This is a very important section of the newspaper. Sometimes there is only one page of editorials or opinions, but some newspapers have an entire section of editorials. The editorial section is the part of the paper where the editors and others give their point of view on important subjects. They may write about events in the news. They may have something good to say about something that has happened. More often, however, editorials criticize the government for its actions. If the President of the United States signs a bill into law, and the editor of the paper feels that the law is bad, he may write an editorial about it. This does not mean that the law will not go into effect. It is just a statement by the editor of the paper about what he or she thinks of the law. The newspapers may influence their readers in this way. In national elections, the newspapers will often have editorials about a particular candidate the editor prefers for the job. The editorials ask the readers to vote for this candidate. Many people may agree with the newspaper and vote for the candidate. The editorials are important because they may affect people in this way. If you want to know the opinion or point of view of the editors of an English language newspaper, you can find out by carefully reading the editorial section.

In some newspapers, people besides the editors write editorials. These people may write for another newspaper, or they may have no connection to any paper. They may agree with the editors or they may disagree with them. In this way, the newspaper may give other points of view and some other opinions, too. *The New York Times* does this on its Op-Ed page. If you read several editorials on the Op-Ed page, you may find several different opinions of something that has happened.

The newspaper is very helpful to anyone who wants to be informed about world developments. It is also helpful to people who want information about sports, or who want to know how they can improve themselves and their lives. Most English language newspapers have some statement of their point of view on developments in the news. You can learn to read English and also learn many interesting things by reading a daily newspaper.

EXERCISES
Comprehension
1. What are the four main ways people learn about news?
2. How is the radio useful in learning about the news?
3. Is an English language newspaper hard to read?
4. How can newspaper advertising help you?
5. What is usually in the first section of the newspaper?
6. Where is the sports news usually printed?
7. Why is there a lot of sports news?
8. What are features?
9. Describe the editorial or opinion section.
10. What is the Op-Ed page?

Discussion
Part A
1. Describe a newspaper from your native country.
2. Do you like to read the newspaper? Why or why not?
3. Do you often read editorials?
Part B
1. Get a copy of *The New York Times* and find each of the sections mentioned here.
2. Get two English language newspapers and compare the two front pages. How are they alike? How do they differ?
3. There are some newspapers which report only one kind of news. Discuss any newspapers of this kind that you know of. Try to find some in the library.

A Sunday *Washington Post*

Directed Sentences

Directions: Make sentences using the following word groups. You may use any form of a given word. You may use the words in any order.

1. features-useful-informative
2. contain-main
3. include-World Cup-Davis Cup
4. daily-influence-actions
5. criticize-editors-editorial-leaders
6. elections-candidate-qualified
7. particular-fix-besides
8. helpful-major-folded
9. nearby-on sale-lower
10. no matter-practice-cause

Suggested Reading

Nash, W. Roy. *How Newspapers Work* (Macmillan, 1974)
Marland, M. *Following the News* (Chatto and Windus, 1967)
Merrill, J., et al., *The Foreign Press* (Louisiana State University Press, 1970)

DATING PATTERNS IN THE USA

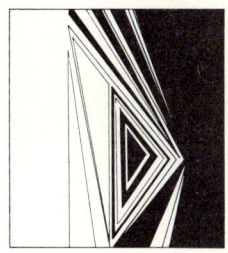 In the United States, in general, young people enjoy a great deal of freedom. They have much more freedom than the young people of many other countries. It is probably also true that American young people have more freedom now than they have ever had before. It is not really clear whether all of this freedom is a good thing with respect to dating relationships. As a result of the freedom that young people have, dating has changed substantially in recent years.

In the traditional dating pattern in the United States, much of the responsibility for a date falls to the young man. In this pattern, the young man must first call the girl he wishes to date on the telephone. Usually, this call is made quite early in a week. Most girls in traditional dating relationships expect to get a telephone call from a young man by Wednesday. Most dating occurs on weekends. Many young people do not have to get up early for school or work on Saturday and Sunday mornings, so Friday nights and Saturday nights are popular nights for dates. The young man must ask the girl for the date, and suggest some things that they might do together. It is usually up to the young man to pay for all of the evening's activities.

There are many things to do on dates. Many young people enjoy going to sports events, such as football and baseball games. These games may occur at a high school, college, or in a large sports arena in a city. A very popular place for young people to go on dates is the movies. Almost everyone enjoys a good movie, and almost every town has at least one movie theater. Young people may also enjoy going to a night club or coffee house. Here, they may listen to music and dance, and perhaps meet some of their friends. These are a few of the things young people do on dates in the United States.

In some parts of the United States, traditional dating relationships begin when young people are in high school. In other places, young people do not go out in couples until they are in college, or in their early twenties. Some young men would rather go out with just one girl all of the time. Every Saturday night, a young man will go out with the same girl. Many girls enjoy this kind of relationship also. It gives both the boy and the girl a chance to get to know one another quite well. Sometimes, this may lead to marriage. Other young people

Robert J. Capece

A traditional date

enjoy dating different individuals. One week they may go out with one person, the next week with another. They get to know many people this way, and may not wish to have a serious relationship with just one person.

Many young people in the United States, especially college students, do not go out on either of these traditional dates. Instead, they go out on group dates. In this kind of dating pattern, small groups of young people go out together. All of the people in the group are usually friends, but some of the people in the group may not know each other. No one young man is with any particular girl. They are all together as part of the group. This is very different from the traditional date.

A group date differs from a traditional date in several ways. First, there are no special relationships in the group. No particular girl and boy are together all the time. Second, the group date may occur on a weekend, but it may not be planned in advance. A group of young people may decide on Saturday afternoon that they want to spend Saturday evening together. They may all decide to go to a movie, or to some other event. On a group date, no one is paired with anyone else. As a result, every person pays for his or her own expenses. This means that the girls must pay for themselves. They must pay their own admission for the movies, for a cup of coffee, or for anything else that costs money during the date.

Many young people find the group date to be a great deal of fun. The young men on a group date are under no pressure. They do not have to be with any particular girl during the evening. They do not have to pay for anyone but themselves. They do not have to be especially polite or formal during the date. Everyone can relax and have a good time. Group dates may lead to serious relationships for some members of the group. Maybe a girl and boy on a group date find that they have a lot in common and enjoy being together. They may spend more time together, with the group, and with each other. But usually, everyone on a group date is just interested in a good time. No one worries about a serious relationship.

The group date may be good for very young people. They may not know what kind of person they like. They may like to spend their time with many different people. But it also does not give young people a chance to have a serious relationship. A serious relationship can help a young person in many ways. A person may learn what is good and what is bad about a serious relationship. Usually, in dating, young people find out what kind of person they would like to marry. If a young person always goes on group dates, there is no chance to find out. As we can see, group dates have their good points and their drawbacks.

The group date is very different from the traditional date, don't you think? Young people in the United States today enjoy both of these types of relationships. Traditional dating relationships give young people a chance to get to know one another quite well. Group dates give young people a chance to get to know many other young people and to have a more relaxed evening. Both kinds of dates have their good points. The group date is a relatively new idea among young people. It seems to be popular for the reasons described here.

EXERCISES
Comprehension
1. Why has dating changed a lot recently?
2. What does a young man have to do on a traditional date?
3. When do most young people go out on dates?
4. Name three things young people may do on dates.
5. At what age do young people begin dating?
6. Describe a group date.
7. Explain how group dates differ from traditional dates.
8. Why are group dates so popular?
9. What is an important drawback of group dates?
10. Why are serious relationships important?

A group date

Discussion
Part A
1. Do you like traditional dates? Why or why not?
2. Do you like group dates? Why or why not?
3. If you are a woman, would you pay for your own expenses on a date? Why or why not?
4. Have you ever gone out on a group date? If so, describe it. If not, would you like to?

Part B
1. Compare dating patterns in the U.S. to those in your country.
2. Do you think that the freedom American young people have is good? Explain your opinion.
3. In this essay, one person's impression of dating patterns in the U.S. is given. If you have been or are in the U.S., do you agree with these impressions?
4. Do you think group dates would be popular in your country? Are they popular now?

Directed Sentences
   Directions: Make sentences using the following word groups. You may use any form of a given word. You may use the words in any order.
1. couples-formal-lead
2. respect-differ-patterns
3. pay-admission-coffee
4. pair-relax
5. cost-baseball
6. night-common-night club-coffee house
7. freedom-drawbacks

Suggested Reading
American magazines such as *Seventeen* and *Cosmopolitan*
Berne, Eric. *Games People Play* (Grove Press, 1964)
Morris, Desmond. *The Naked Ape* (Dell, 1969)

FOOTBALL VS. BASEBALL
An Opinion

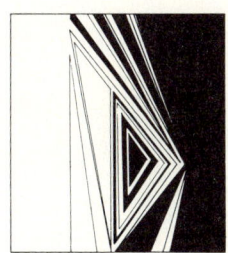

Two sports are very popular in the United States. These sports are football and baseball. Many people enjoy both of these games. Baseball is sometimes called the most popular sport in the United States. Many people think that it is the national sport. But, today, baseball does not seem as popular as football. Football has become more popular in the United States recently. The writer thinks that there are many reasons why football may be more popular now.

Baseball is played by two teams of nine men each. Different men have different jobs when the team is on the field. Each team must try to score more points than the other team. A point is scored when one man hits the ball and then runs around the playing field to each of the four bases.

The men who play baseball must do two things well. First, they must hit the ball when it is their turn. If they can hit the ball well, they can help their team to win the game. Second, they must catch and throw the ball well. When their team is on the field, they can keep the other team from winning. When one team has hit the ball and the hitter is running from one base to another, the players on the second team must try to get the ball and throw it to one of the four bases. If they can throw the ball to base before the hitter can run to it, they get the hitter "out." These are the two abilities that men who play baseball must have to help their team win.

There are problems with baseball. If you have watched a game of baseball, you already know about some of these problems. The game seems to be very slow. There is no time limit on the game so one game may take as much as three hours. Also, for some people, the game is not very interesting. Some Americans complain that there are too many professional baseball teams in America now. There are twenty-four professional teams. With so many teams, more men can play professional baseball. This also means that the men who play professionally are not always the best players. In fact, the writer believes there are really not enough good players to make the game fun. Baseball is played by many amateurs, by college students, and by others, but the professionals are the ones that people care most about. Many people find baseball boring for these reasons.

Of course, there are some good things about baseball. Unlike football, it is easy to understand. You don't have to be very intelligent to play baseball or to

A baseball game

watch it. You can easily understand what is happening on the field. Many Americans enjoy going to a baseball game during the summer months. The weather is warm and usually sunny, and it is a pleasure to sit outside for a few hours and watch a game. Baseball games do not usually cost much money. You can go to a baseball game for a very small amount of money, and still have a very good time.

Football is different from baseball in a number of ways. The writer thinks it is a better game than baseball. Each of the two football teams is made up of twenty-two members. Only eleven men from each team play at any time. When the team has the ball, one group of eleven men play. They try to score a goal, for six or seven points. When the team does not have the ball, the other group of eleven men plays. They try to keep the other team from scoring a goal. Goals are scored in football by carrying or throwing the ball down a long field and past the goal line. This is done with a variety of plays. The team may try to carry the ball or throw the ball in different ways. The team only has four chances to move the ball a certain part of the way to the goal. If the team does not do this, it loses the ball to the other team. The small number of chances the team has to move the ball makes the game exciting.

Some Americans dislike football. They feel that the game is too violent. Many men get hurt during the game. However, they are not usually hurt too seriously. They wear special clothes for protection from being hurt. Football is somewhat more complex than baseball. Some people dislike football because they think it is too hard to understand. But anyone who watches a game carefully should be able to understand most of what happens on the field. Some people think that football, like baseball, has too many professional teams. Since there are twenty-six teams, this may be true. There are new professional football teams too. If they succeed, there will be even more teams. These are a few of the problems of football. In spite of these problems, the writer thinks football is a better game than baseball.

Unlike baseball, football seems to be a fast game. The playing time, the time that the teams are actually moving the football, for each game is about one hour. Because there is only a limited amount of time available, and because each team must move the ball part of the way to the goal every four plays, the game is very interesting. You can watch and try to guess what the team is going to do on each play. After the game is over, many Americans discuss it and decide whether the teams played well or not. This is interesting and fun. The fact that there are many good players who play football also helps to make football a more interesting game than baseball. Football is played for a relatively short time each year. The first games begin in the fall, when the weather begins to get cool. Most teams play until winter. The professional football players begin playing football in August, and their season ends in January. Professional football teams are not the only football teams that people care about. Many important colleges and universities have football teams. These teams are often very good. They are a lot of fun to watch. The college football season generally ends at the end of the year, although a few games are played after New Year's Day. College students and many other people go to football games at different colleges. In major cities, where there are professional teams, many people go to football games also. However, many people prefer to watch football on television.

Football is a very exciting sport, and it is very popular in America now. It seems to be much more interesting and exciting than baseball. The writer enjoys football games much more than baseball games. Both sports are popular, but football is growing in popularity. It may soon be considered America's national sport.

EXERCISES

Comprehension

1. What are two very popular American sports?
2. Describe the game of baseball.
3. What are two important abilities a person must have to play baseball?
4. Describe three problems of baseball.
5. What are some of the good things about baseball?
6. Describe a football team.
7. Why do some Americans dislike football?
8. Is football really hard to understand?
9. Name one problem that professional baseball and professional football share.
10. Why is college football interesting?

A football game

Discussion
Part A
1. Which does the writer like better, football or baseball?
2. How do you know what the writer feels?
3. Is the writer accurate in statements of fact? Or are some of them false?
4. Does the writer seem to be able to change opinion if the inaccuracies are pointed out? Why do you think so?
5. Why do you think this essay is about *only* football and baseball?
Part B
1. Name a sport you enjoy watching. Explain why you like it.
2. Compare two sports that are popular in your country.
3. Does your country have a national sport? What is it?

Suggested Reading
Angell, Roger. *The Summer Game* (Popular Library, 1973)
Bouton, Jim. *Ball Four* (Dell, 1971)
Cope, Myron. *The Game That Was: The Early Days of Pro Football* (World Publishers, 1970

WORD STUDY REVIEW
To the student: These exercises will help you to learn new words in English more easily. Study each part carefully, and review new words from the first fourteen chapters.

A. Noun endings: **-ist, -ian**
The endings *-ist* and *-ian* are added to words when speaking of a person who does or is concerned with the thing mentioned. Add the ending *-ist* or *-ian* to the following words from the first fourteen chapters:
A person who works in biology is a biolog_____
A person who works in chemistry is a chem_____
A person who works with microscopes is a microscop_____
A person concerned with the period when Victoria was queen of England is a Victor_____

Here are some other words you have studied in the last fourteen chapters. Add the necessary ending when speaking of the following:
A person who studies behavior is a behavior_____
A person who studies physiology is a physiolog_____
A person who studies science is a scient_____

B. Combining form: **-logy**
The form *-logy* is added to a word to mean "the study of" "theory of," or "science of." Add the ending *-logy* to the following forms from the first fourteen chapters:
The study of living things is bio_ _____
The study of life processes is physio_____
The study of applied science is techno_____

C. **Usage Practice**
    Directions: Fill in the blank with the correct form of the word in brackets [ ].
1. Charles Darwin was a famous [biology] _____.
2. The study of applied science, [tech-] _____, is helpful to us in many ways.
3. In order to understand pollution, you must know some [bio-] _____.
4. Perhaps you have heard of B. F. Skinner, a professor who is a [behavior] _____.
5. [Chemistry] _____ are interested in the basic things that make up our world.
6. To solve the pollution problem we will need the help of many [science] _____.
7. A person who studies medicine must also be a [physiology] _____.
8. The [Victoria] _____ period was a very interesting period in British history.
9. Much of the exciting work in medical research is done by [microscope] _____.

LASERS

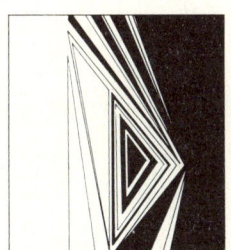 A very interesting and important development in science is a device called the laser. A laser is a machine which produces a light beam. The light produced by a laser is a very special kind of light. The light, called a laser beam, is powerful and can be made to do many things. The laser was first developed in 1960, so this is really quite a new kind of device.

There are many different uses for lasers and several different types have been developed. Some use gases to produce the light beam. The gases are heated and cooled, and these processes cause the gases to produce energy in the form of light. Some lasers use a liquid or a solid, which is heated and then cooled to produce the light. One special feature of lasers is that the light beam can be stored. If the stored light is then suddenly let go, it is extremely powerful. The light from a laser beam can be used either by storing it and letting it go suddenly, or by using it in a continuous stream.

There are three important areas where the control of the laser beam has been put to use by scientists. These areas are industry, communications, and medicine. In each area, the scientists have been able to use the laser to do things that they could not do before. The laser has been very helpful.

In industry, the laser beam has been used for measurement and drilling. When something large is being built—for example, a large airplane—it is important to have very accurate measurements. The laser beam allows accurate measurement of a hundredth of an inch (.25 millimeters) for long distances to 200 feet (sixty meters) or more. This accurate measurement also allows lasers to be helpful in laying down pipelines over long distances. As lasers become more common in industry, there will be more and more uses for them.

In communications, lasers have been especially useful. The light beam can be used to carry many different kinds of communications. The laser has been helpful to scientists in communicating with satellites in space. The laser can carry information from a satellite to a receiving station on earth. Space scientists can also send information to a satellite from the earth. This kind of communication is helpful in taking measurements of the earth's surface, and in predicting weather conditions in different places on earth. In the future, laser beams used with satellites may save lives by predicting earthquakes and hurricanes.

Using a laser

The laser may also be helpful in communications on earth. A laser beam can carry many communication signals at one time. One beam, for example, can carry the broadcasts from seven different television channels. This may make it possible to have many more television channels and make it possible to show many different things on TV. Lasers may be used for telephone communications too, since the beam can carry several telephone conversations at once.

There is one problem in using the laser beam for communications on earth. The problem is that the light beam will not go through rain or snow. Scientists and people who work in communications are trying to solve this problem now. The scientists think they may be able to put the laser beam in some kind of special tube to protect it from the weather. The specialized field of putting lasers in a small tube is called fiber optics. If work in fiber optics is successful, all of our telephone calls and television programs will be sent by laser beam.

The laser is also useful in medicine. The light beam can be focused on a very small point. The beam is made to concentrate on that point. The scientist's ability to do this makes the laser very helpful in working on human cells. A laser beam may be used to cut a cell into two parts or to work on one part of the cell and leave the rest of it alone. A laser may also be used in surgery of different kinds. One of the first uses for the laser was in eye surgery. The laser beam may prove helpful in other kinds of surgery, as well as in research in medicine.

The laser is a very exciting scientific development. It has been used to help people in many ways. The different types of lasers can serve many of people's needs. As scientists become better at using the laser, many new advances will be made, and perhaps many problems which we have not been able to solve will be solved by the use of the laser.

EXERCISES

Comprehension

1. What is a laser?
2. When was the laser first developed?
3. Name the different types of lasers.
4. What is one special feature of the laser?
5. How can the laser be used in industry?
6. How can the laser be used in space communication?
7. How might the laser be helpful in earth communication?
8. What is a problem with using lasers for communication on earth?
9. What is fiber optics?
10. How can the laser be used in medicine?

Discussion

Part A
1. Have you ever seen a laser? Describe one if you have.
2. List some other recent scientific developments which have practical uses.
   Part B
1. If lasers can help with building large things and laying pipelines, discuss some industries where they might be helpful.

2. What are some good and bad things about satellite communications?
3. How might a laser be used in your country?

Directed Sentences

Directions: Make sentences using the following word groups. You may use any form of a given word. You may use the words in any order.

1. energy-device
2. communications-signals-continuous
3. beam-control-surgery
4. processes-heat-liquid-gas-produce
5. satellite-predict-hurricane-conditions
6. laser-tube-fiber optics-protect
7. focused-concentrate-powerful-cell
8. measurement-drilling-lay down-pipelines

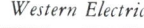
Western Electric

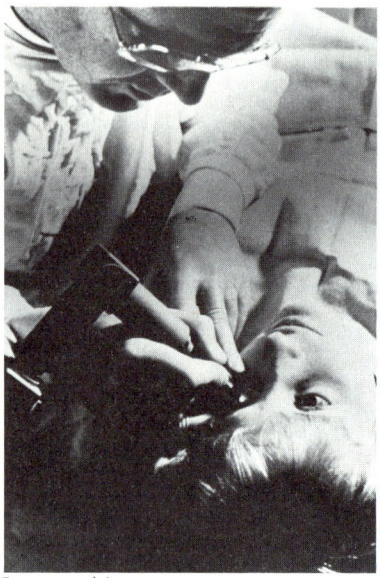
Laser used in eye surgery

Suggested Reading

Barnes, Frank ed. *Laser Theory* (Institute of Electrical and Electronics Engineers, 1970)
Ross, Monte ed. *Laser Applications* (Academic Press, 1971)
Siegman, Anthony E. *An Introduction to Lasers* (McGraw-Hill, 1971)

THE STOCK MARKET II

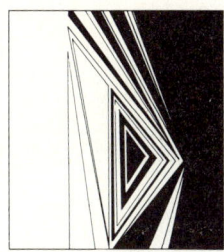 In a previous essay, the basic work of the stock market was described. Some of the reasons why companies go public and some of the reasons why people invest were given. The American stock market is the most closely watched of the markets around the world. There are several reasons for this. The American stock market reflects the economic outlook of most Americans. It also reflects the state of American business in general. The New York Stock Exchange often has an effect on stock markets in other countries. The stock market is also watched for reactions in the United States to international and national news developments. Each of these aspects of the stock market is quite complex.

The way in which the stock market is watched and studied is important and interesting. The American stock market is usually reported to be up or down as compared to the previous day's business. The up or down position of the market is calculated by taking an average of the price changes of a few important stocks. In fact, three averages are calculated. These are called the Dow Jones averages. These are averages of thirty industrial stocks, twenty railroad stocks, and fifteen utility stocks. The averages of these groups of stocks show what is happening in the market generally. Several other averages similar to these are also used. The New York Stock Exchange has its own average of stock prices. In general, if the Dow Jones averages (sometimes called the "Dow") are up, then most stocks are up. If the averages are down (or "off," as they are sometimes said to be), then most stocks are probably down in price compared to the previous day. And whether the American stock markets are up or down in these ways may tell you quite a lot about the general economic outlook.

The American stock market reflects the economic outlook of most Americans. Many of the people who invest in the stock market are small investors. They do not have very much money invested in stocks. Usually, these people buy stock for two reasons. First, if they have extra money which they would like to invest, they are likely to put it into the stock market. Second, when the market is going up, an investor can make money by investing. When economic times are good in the United States, many people may buy small amounts of stock. All of this buying may cause the market to go up, reflecting good times and confidence in the American economy. When times are bad and people are short of money, they are likely to hold on to their money. They may also decide to sell stock they

Edward C. Topple

New York Stock Exchange showing brokers' call board

already own. Both actions give people more money for their own use. In either case, the market will generally go down as a result, reflecting the economic outlook of investors.

The American stock market is also an index of American business. Many of the same things that cause individual investors to buy or sell stock also cause businesses to buy or sell. If times are good and businesses have money, they too may invest in the stock market. In this way, the stock market shows whether the whole economy is doing well or not. Large companies may own large amounts of stock. If a large company buys or sells many shares of a major stock, this may affect the stock of other companies in related fields. A decision to buy or sell stock by one or a few of these large companies may have a very important effect on the market as a whole.

The American stock market has a strong effect on other stock exchanges. There are stock exchanges in many major cities around the world. All of these stock exchanges watch the activity of the two American exchanges. This is because each business all over the world is affected by all other business. It is also because the two American stock exchanges—the New York Stock Exchange and the American Stock Exchange—are two of the largest in the world. Developments on the American exchanges have an effect on developments on other exchanges around the world.

Finally, the stock market is an index of reaction to developments in the news. In the stock exchange in New York, there are special news screens from the international news wire services. When they look at these screens, all the people at the stock exchange know about important news developments. The same news is flashed on screens in brokers' offices. If your broker knows that a news development will influence your stock, he may quickly tell you to buy or sell. People who invest money in the stock market seem to be affected by major news developments. International crises of any kind will usually cause people to sell stock. Usually, the market will go down if many people want to sell their stock. Good business developments—important trade agreements, treaties between countries, and other developments which may make business prosper—are usually received favorably on the stock market. Good news of this kind encourages people to buy stock. Such developments will usually make the stock market go up.

The stock market activity is important to many people. Every hour of a business day, the radio news will include a report on the stock market. Usually, the Dow Jones averages are given, and the stock market is said to be up or down compared to the previous day. These developments are important to everyone from the individual investor to major American and international businesses. It is not surprising that the American stock market is a closely watched economic barometer.

EXERCISES
Comprehension
1. Why are the American stock markets important?
2. How is the up or down position of the market calculated?

3. What are the Dow Jones averages?
4. Explain why the stock market is an index of the economic outlook of the U.S.
5. What economic developments affect both individual and business investments?
6. How can large companies affect the stock market?
7. Why do other stock exchanges watch the American exchanges?
8. What effect does good news usually have on the stock market? Why?
9. What effect does bad news usually have on the stock market? Why?
10. Why are stock market reports given on the news?

Discussion
Part A
1. Why might you need to know about the stock market?
2. Discuss some recent events that may have affected the stock market.
3. Is the stock market in your country affected by major news developments?
Part B
1. (Class or group exercise) Follow a stock listed in the newspaper for a few days. Does the price go up or down? Try to find the Dow Jones averages, and compare your stock to the Dow Jones averages. Try to explain why the stock goes up or down.
2. On the basis of this exercise, are the Dow Jones averages a good index for all stock market activity, or not? Why?

Edward C. Topple

The New York Stock Exchange

Directed Sentences

Directions: Make sentences using the following word groups. You may use any form of a given word. You may use the words in any order.

1. surprise-extra
2. largest-previous-report
3. prosper-confidence-favorably
4. position-Dow Jones-index-economy
5. crises-trade agreements-wire services-flashed
6. strong-reactions-economic-barometer
7. industrial-railroad-utility-reflect-outlook

Suggested Reading

Porter, Sylvia. *The Sylvia Porter Money Book* (Avon Books, 1976)
Smith, Adam. *The Money Game* (Random House, 1968)
The Wall Street Journal

THREE KINDS OF FOOTBALL

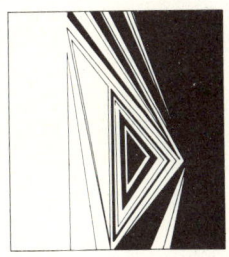 There are three popular team games which are similar. They are soccer, rugby, and American football. The games are similar because, in all of them, a ball is used and the players move the ball with their bodies, especially their feet. However, each game is different from the others in a number of ways. The games differ in their origins, in their rules and strategies, in where they are played, and in many other ways.

Soccer may be the most popular of the three games. It is played in many countries around the world. Soccer is also called association football. The modern form of the game was first played in Great Britain in the nineteenth century. The first international soccer competition was a game between England and Scotland in 1872. Soccer is one of the team sports played in the Olympics. It has been a regular part of the Olympic games since 1908.

Another important international soccer competition is called the World Cup. The World Cup competition occurs once every four years. It is usually played between the Olympics. A World Cup soccer match is held two years after the Olympics. The players in the World Cup are professionals, while those who play in the Olympics must be amateurs. The winner of the World Cup match is considered the world champion soccer team.

Soccer is played by two teams with eleven men on each team. Each team has two ways to win. It must score more goals than the other team, and it must prevent the other team from scoring goals. Each goal in soccer is worth one point. Soccer is played with a round ball. The ball may be kicked, or it may be moved by any part of the body except the hands. Ten of the players must not use their hands. Only one player is allowed to use his hands. This is the player who defends the goal, or the "goalie" on the team.

A soccer game usually lasts for ninety minutes. The playing time is divided into two equal parts. The teams play for forty-five minutes, and then take a short rest. After this half-time rest, they play again for another forty-five minutes. Soccer is tiring because the game is very long. To help the players have some rest during the game, there are other players who may play for them. These players substitute for other players so that everyone may have some rest during the game.

Rugby

The second of the three types of football is called rugby. It is played professionally in only a few countries. The most important professional teams are in Great Britain, France, Australia, and New Zealand. When rugby is played by professional players, it is called Rugby League. Other people play rugby too. Amateur rugby is called Rugby Union. There are somewhat different rules for Rugby Union and Rugby League.

Like soccer, modern rugby began in Great Britain in the nineteenth century. It was played by many people in the countries of the British Empire, and was quite popular. Now, it is not so popular. It is not part of the Olympics. The countries that have professional rugby teams have an occasional competition to decide the best team. They do not have regular World Cup competition such as there is for soccer.

The major difference between rugby and soccer is that rugby players may use their hands to move the ball. The shape of the ball is oval rather than round as it is in soccer. Rugby is also different from soccer in that it is played by a larger number of players. An amateur rugby team has fifteen players, while a professional team has thirteen.

A rugby game usually lasts for eighty minutes. The playing time is divided equally into two halves. Rugby teams also have substitutes just as soccer teams do. This helps all the players by giving them a chance to rest during the games. Rugby is somewhat more complex than soccer. It may be easy to follow when you are watching it, but it is hard to explain.

The scoring of a rugby game, for example, is complicated. There are three ways to score points in rugby. The first way to score points in rugby is through "tries." A "try" happens when a member of the team touches the ball down over the opponents' goal line. A try is worth three points. After a try has been scored, a goal may be attempted. This goal is scored by kicking the ball over the goal line from a particular place on the field. The goal is worth two points. A third way of scoring points in rugby is by scoring a field goal. A team can get three points by kicking the ball through the goal from anywhere on the field. Each team in a rugby game tries to score more points than the other team. Each team tries to keep the other team from scoring. The team with more points at the end of the game wins.

American football is also a complicated game. It is a cross between soccer and rugby. This means that it is like soccer in some ways and like rugby in other ways. It is like soccer, for example, because there are eleven men on each team. It is also like rugby because an oval ball is used to play the game. However, there is a difference between the oval ball used in rugby and the one used in American football. The American football is pointed at the ends, but the rugby football is not.

American football has the same basic origin as rugby and soccer. When the people of Great Britain came to settle in the United States, they brought soccer and rugby with them. American football has developed into a somewhat different game, however, as a result of the work of a man named Walter Camp. Camp worked on the American Football Rules Committee between 1880 and 1913. He helped to make so many changes in the game that he is sometimes called the "Father of American Football."

Modern American football is different from rugby and soccer in many ways. Although only eleven men play on a football team at one time, there are actually twenty-two players. In modern football, most teams have two groups of eleven men. One group, the offense, plays when the team has the ball, and the other group, the defense, plays when the other team has the ball. This arrangement allows the players to specialize in one aspect of the game. Some players are very good at defense, and others are much better at scoring goals. All of the players play in the part of the game that they do best.

An American football game lasts for sixty minutes, plus all the time the ball is not actually "in play." The playing time is usually divided into four equal periods of fifteen minutes. The players get a short rest between periods. But after two periods, they get a minimum of fifteen minutes' rest. Scoring in American football is very complicated. A team may earn six points by throwing or carrying the ball over the opposing team's goal line. After the goal, the team has an opportunity to score another point or two. It may score another point by kicking the ball through the goal posts. The team may score two points by carrying the ball over the goal line again. A team may also score three points in American football by kicking the ball from the playing field through the goal posts during regular play. This is called a field goal.

Of course, these are general statements. Each of these football games is much more complex. There is a great deal of strategy involved in the play of each game. All the players must be very strong and intelligent. They must think clearly under the pressure of competition, and they must remember the many different plans their team has for scoring. Soccer is an internationally popular sport which is played in many countries around the world. Rugby is played in a few countries. It is very popular in the countries where it is played. American football is played in the United States, and a similar form is played in Canada. All of the games are somewhat similar, but each one also has unique characteristics.

EXERCISES
Comprehension
  1. How are soccer, rugby, and American football similar?
  2. Describe the origins of soccer.
  3. What is the World Cup?
  4. Explain how soccer is played.
  5. What is the difference between Rugby League and Rugby Union?
  6. How is rugby different from soccer?
  7. Describe the scoring in rugby.
  8. How is American football different from both soccer and rugby?
  9. Who was Walter Camp?
  10. Explain how American football is played.

World Cup Soccer

Discussion

Part A

1. Why do you think soccer is the most popular of the three games?
2. Which of the three games do you think is most interesting? Why?
3. If you play one of these games, explain some of the strategy used by your team.

Part B

1. Soccer has been described as a violent game. So has American football. Do you agree with this description? Why or why not?
2. Soccer is becoming very popular in the United States. Can you explain why?
3. Describe some other sports you know of that are similar to each other. Where are they played? Explain the similarities.

Directed Sentences

Directions: Make sentences using the following word groups. You may use any form of a given word. You may use the words in any order.

1. half-time—once—champion
2. except-occasional
3. British Empire-settle-origins
4. oval-shape-association football-rugby-difference

5. specialize-opportunity-players
6. strategy-defense-offense-unique
7. worth-goalie-prevent-opponents
8. Rugby Union-Rugby League
9. arrangement-complicated-oppose
10. equal-touch

Suggested Reading

Glanville, Brian. *A History of the Soccer World Cup* (Macmillan, 1974)

Magoun, Francis. *History of Football from the Beginnings to 1871* (Johnson Reprints, 1938)

LEARNING A LANGUAGE

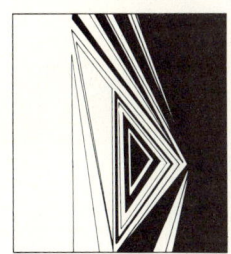 In the second chapter, you read about the field of study called linguistics. Linguists are interested in the abilities to understand and use language that people have. One of the abilities that people have is the ability to learn language. You are using this ability right now in your efforts to learn English as a second language. Most students would like to know how to learn a language more easily. Most linguists and language teachers would also like to know this. Linguists are working on this problem in two ways. First, they are trying to understand how children learn to speak and understand their native language. They are also trying to learn how people learn a second language.

Linguists are not sure how children learn to speak. Some linguists think that children are born with an ability to learn and use a language. This does not mean that you came into the world knowing your native language. It means that, along with many other things, you were born with the ability to learn your native language. One group of linguists feels that with just a little exposure to language, and a little help from your parents, you were able to learn to speak. Another group of linguists does not think this is correct.

This second group of linguists thinks that childern learn to use a language from their parents. They believe that a child's parents teach their child to say sounds and words in their language. When the child knows some words, the parents begin to teach their child to say sentences. The linguists do not think that parents teach their children in the same way that people are taught a second language. Instead, parents probably teach their children by talking to them and correcting their use of language. These linguists feel that you learn your language mainly from your environment. In this case, your environment is your family and your home. As you see, the first group of linguists disagrees.

There are some other theories about how children learn language. Many people are studying the process of language learning by children. This work is being done in many countries. Linguists are not the only people who are interested in these questions. Many psychologists, doctors, and parents are also interested. People who teach foreign languages are interested in this process, too.

Hugh Rogers/Monkmeyer

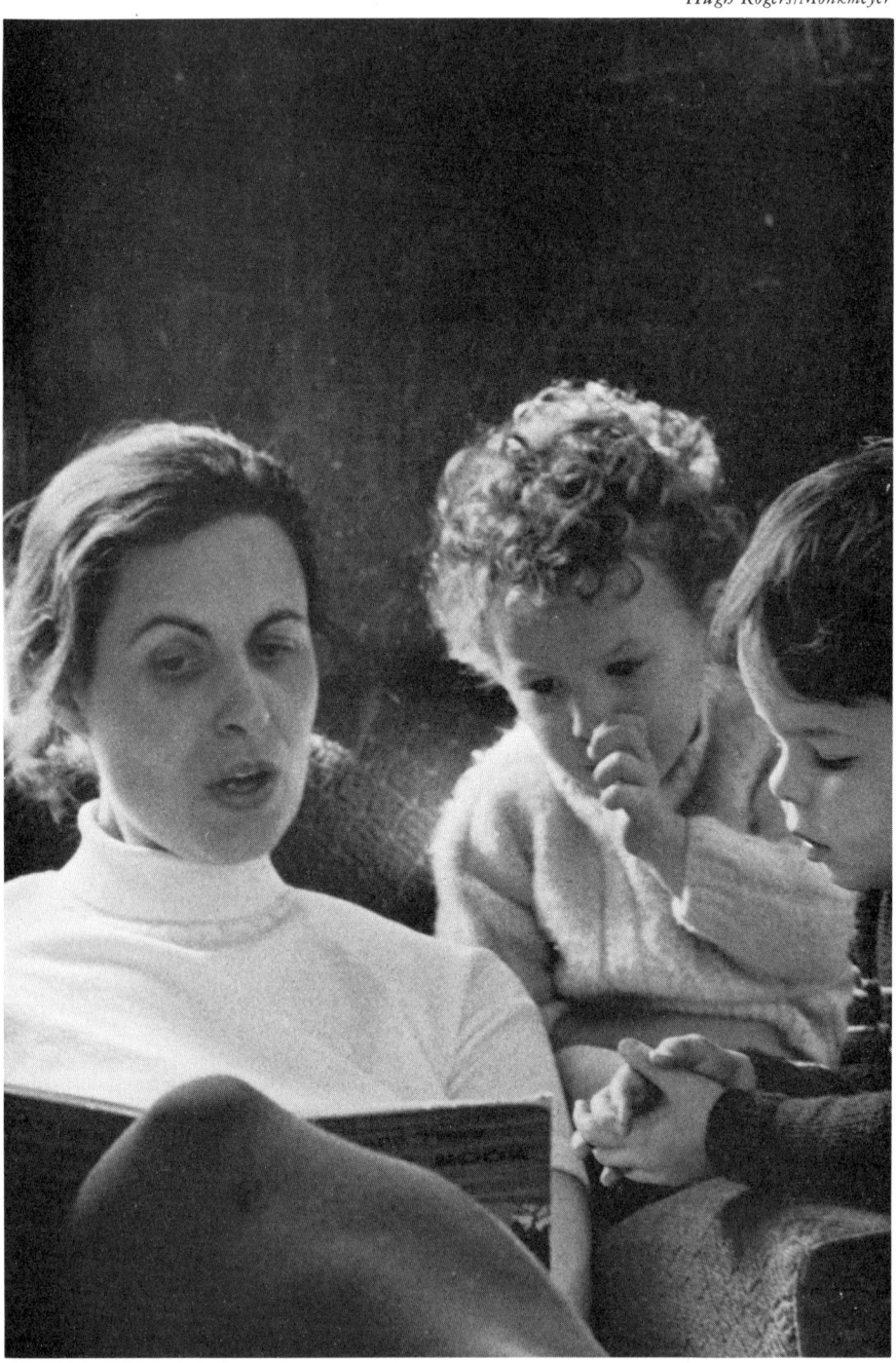

Children learning language from a parent

Foreign language teachers are interested in how children learn to speak their native language for a very important reason. If we knew how children learn their native language, perhaps we would have an easy way to teach adults, as well as children, a second language. This is a very interesting idea. Some foreign language teachers believe that adults learn a second language the same way children learn their native language. These teachers try to make their students' lives similar to the life of a child just learning to speak. These teachers speak only the foreign language in the classroom. They will not speak to the student in the native language. They try to expose the student to as much of the spoken language as possible. They do not teach the student any rules for using the language. Most parents don't teach their children rules for language usage, either. They simply tell the child how to say something correctly. Foreign language teachers using this spoken language method do the same thing. For some students, this method is successful. They learn to speak quickly and easily. They seem to enjoy using the language, and they do not worry about using exactly the right rule for everything they say. Some students, however, cannot learn a language this way. Linguists are trying to find another way to teach them a language.

A second method, the rule-learning method, sometimes works better with these students. Some linguists believe that learning a foreign language is different from learning to speak your native language. They feel that a student must learn the rules for using the language by memorizing them. The students must practice saying things in the language, using the rules correctly. These linguists try to teach the students the rules of the language they want to learn. Then they give the students many sentences in the language to say over and over again. The students are encouraged to make up new sentences using the rules that they have learned and other words that they know.

Some students are very successful with this second, rule-learning method. They learn the language quite quickly and can use it well. They know the rules for using the language, and can speak it and understand it too. For many students, this is the best way to learn a foreign language. For some students, both of these methods may work. Sometimes teachers use a combination of these methods in a class, hoping that everyone will be able to learn the language with one method or the other. Some people can go to a country and "pick up" the language simply from hearing it and trying to communicate. These people are rare.

Most people try to learn a language by taking classes and studying it in some way. Most teachers will try different ways of teaching to help the students learn the language quickly and easily. Linguists and psychologists are trying to understand how people learn and use a language. Perhaps language learning will be easier for everyone when we have a clear understanding of how people learn and use language.

EXERCISES
Comprehension
1. What do linguists do?
2. How are linguists working on the problem of language learning?

3. How do some linguists think children learn to speak?
4. What do other linguists think about children's language learning?
5. Besides linguists, who else is interested in language learning?
6. What is the connection between children's language learning and the language learning of adults?
7. Describe the spoken language method.
8. Describe the rule-learning method.
9. Do all students learn best with only one of these methods?
10. How do teachers use these methods?

Discussion

Part A

1. Try to describe the way English is taught in your class. Which method is used, or is some combination of them used?
2. Which of the two methods described in the essay do you like best? Why?
3. Is language learning easy or hard for you? Try to explain why.
4. What is your goal in learning a foreign language?

Part B

1. If you could tell foreign language teachers how to teach, what would you say?
2. Do you think native language learning and foreign language learning are the same or different? Why?
3. How do *you* think language is learned?

Michael Hardy/Woodfin, Camp

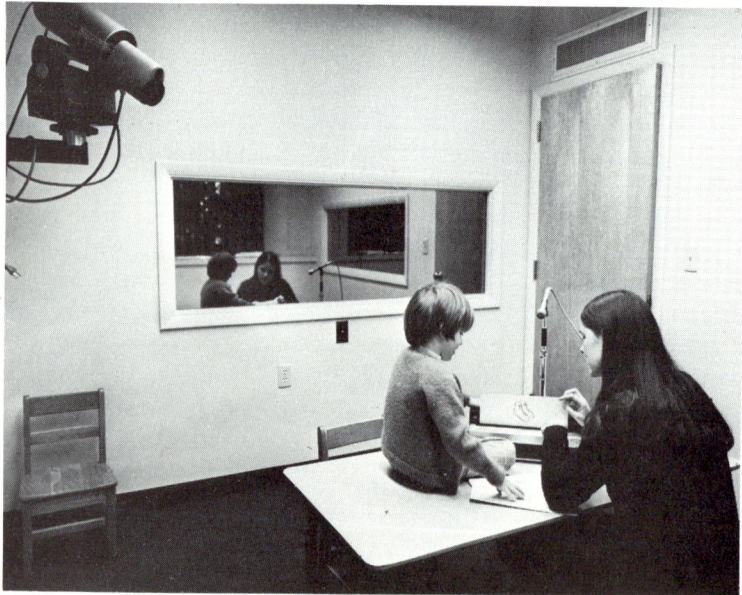

Studying a child learning a language

Directed Sentences

Directions: Make sentences using the following word groups. You may use any form of a given word. You may use the words in any order.

1. efforts-memorize-usage
2. second language-sounds-similar
3. environment-disagree-exposure
4. psychologists-method-successful
5. foreign language-quickly-easily-rare

Suggested Reading

Allen, Harold, and Russell Campbell, eds. *Teaching English as a Second Language* (McGraw-Hill, 1972)

Chastain, Kenneth. *Theory to Practice: The Development of Foreign Language Skills* (Rand McNally, 1976)

Language Learning

THE USES OF SCIENCE

An Opinion

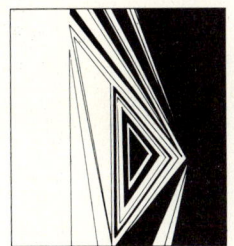

You may have noted that a number of essays in this book are about science. The writer feels that, in general, science is an important and interesting area of study. Some students may have a difficult time studying science, and try not to take science classes. Other students think science classes are boring and have no use. But the writer thinks that everyone needs to know something about science.

Science is important to most people living in the modern world for a number of reasons. In particular, science is important to world peace and understanding, to the understanding of technology, and to our understanding of the natural world. Science is also an interesting area of study for a number of reasons. Some areas of science are especially interesting because they deal with questions all men and women ask themselves. Scientists try to provide some explanations for what happens to people.

Science is important to world peace in many ways. On one hand, scientists have helped to develop many of the modern tools of war. On the other hand, they have also helped to keep the peace through study and research which has improved life for people everywhere. In our time, scientists have been able to help us understand the problem of supplying the world with enough energy. They have begun to develop a number of solutions to the energy problem, for example, using energy from the sun and from the atom. Scientists have also analysed the world's resources. We are going to have to learn to share the resources we have, and we can begin to do this with the knowledge provided to us by science.

Science is also important to everyone who is affected by modern technology. Many of the things that make our lives easier and better are the result of advances in technology. Almost everything in the world has been improved or changed in the last hundred years as a result of technology. While some people would ask whether all these changes are good, it is still true that technology affects all of us. And, if the present patterns continue, technology will affect us even more in the future than it does now. In some cases, such as the technology for taking salt out of ocean water, technology may be essential to our lives on earth. In order to understand the modern world and developments in it in the next century, an understanding of science and technology will be necessary.

Grumman Energy Systems, Inc.

Using energy from the sun to heat a house

The study of science also provides us with an understanding of the natural world. Scientists are learning to predict such things as earthquakes. This may someday help to save hundreds of lives. Scientists are also continuing to study many other natural events such as storms of various kinds. Scientists are also studying people. They are trying to understand not only what makes people human, but also the things that affect people such as illness. They are studying various other aspects of human biology, also. The study of the natural world by scientists and by students of science may help to make the world easier to understand. It may also save many lives, and improve life for many people all over the world.

Some of the things one might study in a science course are extremely interesting questions about people and their lives. Some of these questions are: What are men and women, essentially? What information would help us to understand all people better? What information can explain where human beings come from and why they act the way they do? Questions like these have led biologists to understand the origin and development of the human race. Some of the other questions biologists study have to do with illness. What makes people sick? Why do some people never get sick? Why can some people live to be 100 years old, while others do not live past 55? These are all questions that interest scientists and that, when answered, will surely have an effect on our lives.

One of the reasons science is hard to study is that there are so many questions without answers. Much of science involves asking questions, and then studying and doing research to try to find the answers. Some questions have been studied by research scientists for many years, and the answers are still not known. However, scientists are slowly but surely able to answer more and more questions about life, and these answers change our lives and also explain them.

All of the many different kinds of science are important and interesting. Scientists are asking and answering many interesting and important questions about people and their lives. A basic knowledge of science can help you to understand both the questions and the answers. In the modern world, this ability is essential for everyone.

EXERCISES

Comprehension

1. Explain the writer's view about science.
2. How have scientists contributed to world peace?
3. What are the contributions of technology?
4. What is the value of being able to predict earthquakes?
5. What other natural phenomena are scientists studying?
6. Why do many scientists study human beings?
7. What have biologists contributed to our knowledge of humanity?
8. Why is science hard to study?
9. Why does the writer think that science is important?
10. Why does the writer think that science is interesting?

Ellis Herwig/Stock, Boston

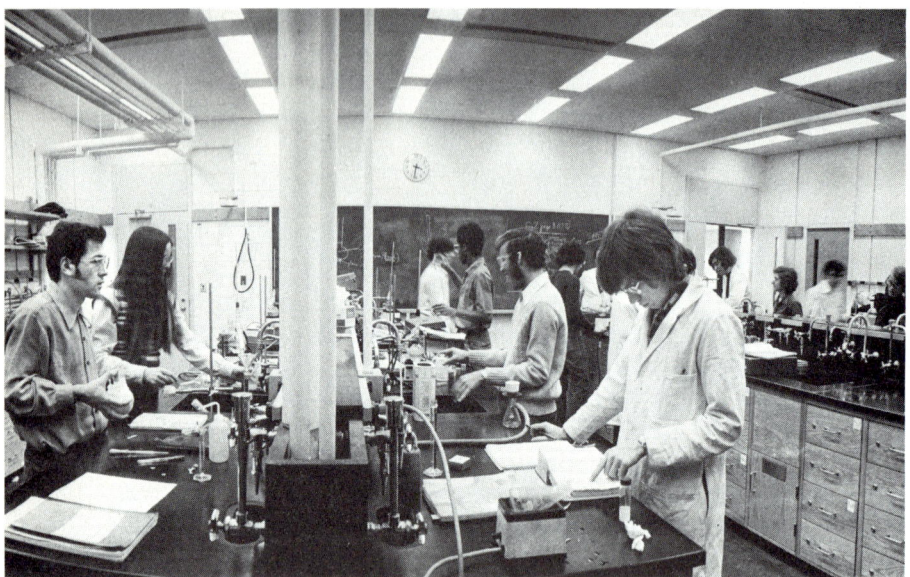

In a science course

Discussion
Part A
1. What is the writer's opinion about science?
2. Compare the writer's opinion with your own.
3. Explain how the writer tries to make you see that science is important to everyone.

Part B
1. How do you feel about science as an area of study?
2. If you are a scientist, explain how your area of science has contributed to human life.
3. If you have not studied much science, explain why not.
4. List some of the most important problems scientists have been studying recently.

Suggested Reading
Eiseley, Loren. *The Unexpected Universe* (Harcourt Brace, 1969)
Sullivan, John. *The Limitations of Science* (Folcroft, 1933)
Vergara, William. *Science in the World Around Us* (Harper & Row, 1975)

WORD STUDY REVIEW
To the student: These exercises will help you to learn new words in English more easily. Study each part carefully, and review new words from the first nineteen chapters.

A. Adjective ending: **-ic**
The ending *-ic* is added to words to make adjectives meaning "of" or "having to do with." Add the ending *-ic* to the following words from the first nineteen chapters:

academy-academ_____   economy-econom_____
characterize-characterist_____   real-realist_____
                              specify-specif_____

B. Verb ending: **-ize**
The ending *-ize* is added to words to make verbs meaning "to cause to be" or "to become like." Add the ending *-ize* to the following words from the first nineteen chapters:

general-general_____   summary-summar_____
special-special_____   system-systemat_____

C. Noun ending: **-ment**
The ending *-ment* is added to words to make nouns meaning "the act of" or "a result of." Add the ending *-ment* to the following words from the first nineteen chapters:

achieve-achieve_____   invest-invest_____
arrange-arrange_____   measure-measure_____
develop-develop_____

D. **Usage Practice**
Directions: Fill in the blank with the correct form of the word given in brackets [ ].

1. The ability to [general] _____ is an important ability in language learning.
2. Winning the Nobel Prize is a great [achieve] _____.
3. Many people are interested in the unique [characterize] _____ of the human race.
4. [Economy] _____ problems are often in the news.
5. Most scientists [special] _____ in some particular kind of science.
6. Everyone would like to find a [real] _____ solution to the problem.
7. Understanding the atom was an important [develop] _____ in science.
8. Do you think that stocks are a good [invest] _____?
9. Binomial nomenclature [system] _____ names for plants and animals in biology.
10. You can take [measure] _____ in the metric or the current U.S. system.

RECENT HISTORY OF MEDICINE

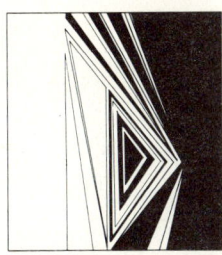 As with the other areas of science discussed in this book, medicine has a long and complicated history. In the present century, there have been important developments in three fields in medicine: chemotherapy, immunology, and endocrinology. Of course, there have also been important developments in many other aspects of medicine. However, some of the most interesting recent developments have occurred in these three fields.

Chemotherapy concerns the use of chemicals or drugs to treat diseases. The main idea in chemotherapy is that certain chemicals will affect a part of the body or the bacteria that causes disease. Before chemotherapy could develop, much had to be known about the human body. Scientists had to know what the parts of the body were before they could know which parts of the body might be affected by a drug. Also, scientists had to know about physiology. Finally, they had to understand the cause and nature of the diseases that affect human beings. In fact, all of these things had already been studied in earlier centuries. Chemotherapy was able to develop as a result of the history of medicine.

Two important advances in chemotherapy occurred during the twentieth century. The first of these has to do with the use of sulfa drugs. These drugs were discovered by Gerhard Domagk, a German scientist, and Leonard Coleman, an English scientist. The sulfa drugs were found to be helpful against several different kinds of diseases, one of which was pneumonia. These drugs were found and first put into use in the 1930's.

The second major advance in chemotherapy involves the development of antibiotics. Antibiotics are chemicals produced by microorganisms or fungi. These chemicals help cure many diseases. The first and most important antibiotic was found by Alexander Fleming in 1928. This is the drug known as penicillin. Penicillin was developed further by Howard Florey and other scientists at Oxford University in England. Penicillin was found to have a variety of uses in curing many different kinds of diseases. However, penicillin did not cure all kinds of diseases. Other antibiotics were developed after penicillin was found to be ineffective in some cases. The new antibiotics helped to cure many other diseases that could not be cured with penicillin.

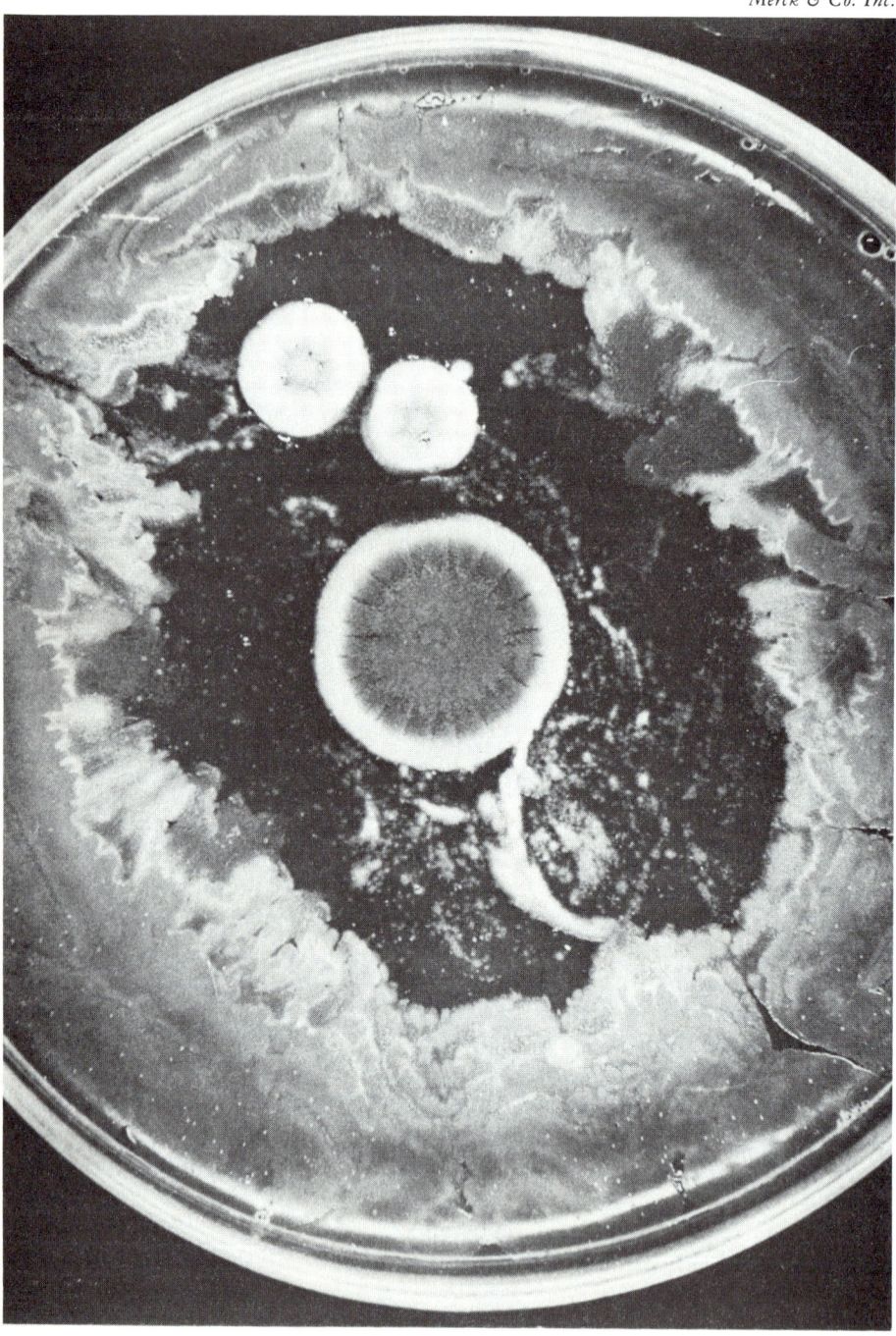

Penicillin

Immunology is a second area of medicine where important developments have occurred. Immunology is the study of immunity, or a person's ability to resist disease. Immunology is partly concerned with producing immunity to certain specific diseases. This area of study has been very rewarding to scientists. Many vaccines have been developed which encourage the human body to produce immunity. Usually, the vaccine causes the body to protect itself from the disease.

A good example of a disease for which a vaccine has been developed is polio. Actually, two vaccines for polio have been developed. The first one was the result of much work by Dr. Jonas Salk, and was called the Salk vaccine. Dr. Salk's vaccine came into general use in 1954. The vaccine successfully prevented those who took it from getting polio. In 1960, a second polio vaccine was developed by Dr. Albert Sabin. The Sabin vaccine was better than the Salk vaccine because it could be given by mouth, while the Salk vaccine had to be given by injection. Many people do not like to take an injection. Many other diseases are no longer common in humans as a result of the development of vaccines. Such diseases as smallpox and typhoid are no longer common because most people have been protected from them by vaccines.

Immunology is also concerned with other aspects of medicine. Most people have some immunity to colds and some other illnesses. However, one disease that affects only a few people is the result of a complete lack of immunity. People with this disease, called immuno-deficiency, have no immunity at all. Children who are born this way must live in special germ-free areas. The cause of this lack of immunity is not yet fully understood. Once it is understood, we will probably also have learned much more about the body's system for immunity.

Another concern of immunology is the relatively new problem of organ transplants. Part of the body's immunity system can cause it to reject a transplanted organ such as a kidney. Many recent transplants have not been successful because of this phenomenon. Scientists are trying to understand how the body's immunity system causes it to reject a transplanted organ. If they can understand this process, they may be able to make organ transplants much more successful. They may be able to keep the body from rejecting a transplanted organ.

A third area of medicine which has had major advances recently is the field of endocrinology. Endocrinology is the study of the endocrine system in the body. This is the system of glands and other organs that produce chemicals called hormones. Hormones are necessary for good health, as they cause necessary reactions of many kinds in the body.

A major development in endocrinology was the discovery of insulin in 1921. Insulin is a hormone produced by the pancreas. It is necessary for correct use of sugar by the body. When insulin is not produced, a person gets a very serious disease called diabetes. Scientists have learned how to make insulin outside the body. Doctors can help people who have diabetes by giving them the insulin they need.

A second area of success in endocrinology was the understanding of sex hormones. This understanding led to the development of the oral contraceptive pill for women. This pill has changed the lives of many people, and may affect all of us. It may allow us to control the number of people on the earth.

In general, all of the work done in the twentieth century in these areas has improved life for many people. Many scientists in these fields now feel that their main concern is keeping people healthy. They are less concerned with curing diseases that people already have. Much work still remains to be done. All of the successful work described here provides great hope for the future.

EXERCISES
Comprehension

1. Are chemotherapy, immunology, and endocrinology the only areas where important developments have occurred recently?
2. What is chemotherapy?
3. What must scientists know about the body for chemotherapy?
4. What are antibiotics?
5. Who was Alexander Fleming?
6. What is immunology?
7. Explain what the Salk and Sabin vaccines do.
8. Why must some children live in germ-free areas?
9. What is endocrinology?
10. How have developments in the three areas mentioned changed medicine?

Mrs. Lindsey Lampp/Baylor College of Medicine

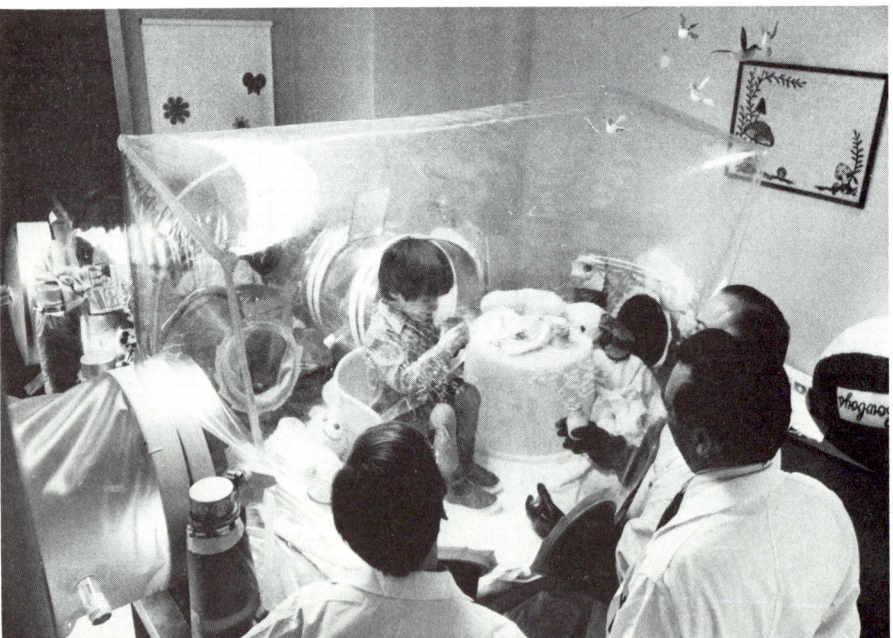

Child in a special germ-free area

Discussion

Part A

1. How is the history of medicine important to modern medicine?
2. Have you ever taken an antibiotic? Explain what happened.
3. What vaccines have you had? Why are they important to everyone?

Part B

1. The developments described here have made it possible for many people to live longer. Is this good or bad in your opinion? Why?
2. Organ transplants are new in medicine. What other organs besides the kidney have been transplanted? Would you give one of your organs (a kidney, for example) to someone else? Why or why not?
3. Do you think the oral contraceptive pill will affect the number of people on earth? Do you think it should? Explain your point of view.

Directed Sentences

Directions: Make sentences using the following word groups. You may use any form of a given word. You may use the words in any order.

1. germ-free—immunity—immuno-deficiency
2. diabetes-lack-insulin-pancreas
3. endocrinology-sex hormones-oral contraceptive pill
4. hormones-chemicals-endocrine-glands
5. vaccines-polio-smallpox-typhoid
6. injection-ineffective-treat
7. chemotherapy-sulfa drugs-penicillin-pneumonia
8. disease-microorganisms-fungi-bacteria
9. antibiotics-drugs-cure
10. kidney-organ-transplants
11. immunology-reject

Suggested Reading

Bishop, Jerry. *New Horizons in Medicine* (Dow Jones Books, 1966)
DiCyan, Erwin. *Vitamins in Your Life* (Simon and Schuster, 1974)
Nolen, William. *Spare Parts for the Human Body* (Random House, 1971)

WOMEN'S LIBERATION

Have you heard of the women's liberation movement? It began in the 1960s. It was started by women who were concerned about their identity, their role in society, and their work, and about the view of women that many people held. Now many American women are deeply concerned about these things. These women would like better and more interesting lives for all women everywhere.

There are many aspects of the women's liberation movement. Some women agree with all of the goals of women's liberation. They want full equality with men in every aspect of life. In marriage, they want husbands and wives to share all of the work and responsibilities of a home and family. In work, they want women and men to have the same jobs and the same chance to succeed. They want women to be paid just as much as men are for the same work. Other women agree with some of the ideas of women's liberation. They want the same pay if they hold the same job as a man. At home, however, they do not expect their husbands to share in the cleaning, cooking, and other household jobs.

It is important to remember that the women's liberation movement is not concerned only with concrete issues. The movement is also concerned with attitudes and beliefs. One example of this concern is the issue of a woman's identity. A woman's identity is what she thinks of herself as a person, who she thinks she is, and what she thinks she can do. Some women do not think they are capable of doing anything important. The women's liberation movement would like to help these women improve their view of themselves. Many women who are concerned with women's liberation have taken jobs, have helped others, have raised healthy children, and have done many other things to contribute to their communities. They have shown that they are capable of being good leaders and of doing many important things.

A second issue of the women's liberation movement is the question of women's roles. Should a woman work outside the home? Should she work if she is married and has children? Or should she stay home to take care of her husband and children? What will the rest of society think of her if she enters a profession or has a career? What will other people think if she wants to stay home and raise a family? These questions do not have just one correct answer. Every woman

Michael Heron/Monkmeyer

A father taking care of the baby

must decide her own role. The women's liberation movement is trying to make it possible for a woman to decide what she wants to do. The movement also wants to make it possible for her to do the best and the most she possibly can.

If a woman decides to take a job outside the home, there are many important questions which are raised. Can she get any job she is capable of and qualified for? Or are some jobs closed to her because she is a woman? If she gets a job and some of her fellow workers are men doing the same work, will she be paid as much as they are? This issue is considered important in the United States. The government has passed some laws to try to help women get any job for which they are qualified, and to help them get the same pay as a man for doing the same work. The government has also passed a law to encourage businesses that get money from the government to be fair to women and minority groups. This is called the Affirmative Action law. It says that if a company is not fair to women and other minority groups, the government will not do business with that company. This encourages businesses to provide equal opportunity for women.

Many people agree with the ideas and goals of women's liberation. They feel that women ought to be considered equal to men in every way. They feel that a woman should be able to decide to stay home and raise a family, or to stay home and not raise a family, or to go out and work, or to have a job outside the home and a family as well. They feel a woman should be able to do anything that she wants to do and can do. Other people are opposed to women's liberation. They do not think that women should have the same jobs and the same pay as men. They believe that men should do all of the important work. They feel that women belong at home, taking care of men and children. Many husbands do not want their wives to work outside the home. Some women agree with these men. People who believe in women's liberation do not feel that it is bad for a woman to remain at home if she wants to. They believe that work in the home is important and should be respected. But they want to make sure that a woman works at home because she wants to, and not because she can't get a job outside the home, or because she does not believe that she can do anything useful in her community.

The women's liberation movement is trying to give women a chance to show what they can do. Perhaps a woman will find the cure for our most serious disease. Perhaps a woman will solve the energy crisis. Perhaps women and men, working together, will be able to accomplish important things better and sooner than men would if men were working alone. If the women's liberation movement is successful, we will have a chance to find out.

Each man and each woman must decide whether he or she agrees with the ideas of the women's liberation movement completely, partly, or not at all. Whether you agree or disagree with women's liberation, you know that it has begun to change our lives.

EXERCISES
Comprehension
1. What is the women's liberation movement?
2. Does everyone have the same attitude about women's liberation?

3. What is a woman's identity?
4. How have women shown that they are capable of doing many things?
5. Explain the issue of women's roles.
6. If a woman works outside the home, what are some of the problems she must solve?
7. What is Affirmative Action?
8. Explain the view of people who agree with women's liberation.
9. Explain the view of people who disagree with women's liberation.

Discussion
Part A
1. Do you agree or disagree with women's liberation? Explain.
2. Do you think Affirmative Action is a good idea? Why or why not?
3. Should women work outside the home?
4. Are the ideas of women's liberation important in your country now?
Part B
1. How might women's liberation affect your life?
2. If you are a man, would you want to be married to a liberated woman?
3. Why do you think some women do not think they are capable of doing anything important?
4. Do you hope that the women's liberation movement is successful? Explain your point of view.

Leif Skoogfors/Woodfin, Camp

Women of the Women's Liberation Movement

Directed Sentences

Directions: Make sentences using the following word groups. You may use any form of a given word. You may use the words in any order.

1. respected-accomplish-succeed
2. issues-attitudes-beliefs-identity
3. capable-goal-cure
4. Affirmative Action-permit-minority group-qualified
5. entitled-equality-fellow workers-liberation
6. movement-career-profession-household

Suggested Reading

de Beauvoir, Simone. *The Second Sex* (Knopf, 1953)
Friedan, Betty. *The Feminine Mystique* (Norton, 1974)
Greer, Germaine. *The Female Eunuch* (McGraw-Hill, 1971)
Millett, Kate. *Sexual Politics* (Avon, 1971)
Ms. magazine

INTERNATIONAL FINANCE

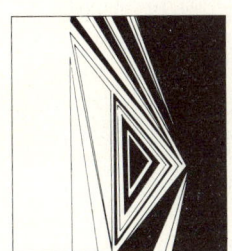 If you have ever traveled outside your native country, you have already had some contact with the complex world of international finance. In your travels, it was probably necessary for you to change your own country's money for the money of the country you were visiting. You may have exchanged money at a bank or at an office of a tourist agency such as Thomas Cook's. Wherever you went, exchanging money put you in touch with international finance. International finance is partly concerned with exchange rates between the monies of various countries. International finance is also concerned with the money system underlying the exchange rates. The development of this system will be described here.

In the years before World War I, most countries were on an international finance system called the gold standard. This system was the result of the general use of gold bullion and coins in trade. Gold was widely used because it was inherently valuable. In the gold standard system, all currencies were valued in terms of gold. If people with one national currency wanted to pay for something in another currency, they had to change their money into the other money. This could easily be done by figuring the relative value of the two currencies in gold. One currency could then be exchanged for the other. This probably sounds like a very good and simple system, but in fact it was neither good nor simple.

For one thing, the gold standard was not a formal agreement among the countries that traded together. Informally, most countries agreed on the gold standard, but if one country did not, many problems resulted. To solve these problems, an international agreement was needed concerning the relative values of the different currencies.

Just before World War I a rise of nationalism developed. Each country felt that its own problems were more important than foreign problems. Each country was intensely concerned with itself. Also, during the war, there was a great deal of inflation. In each country, prices of goods and services rose during and just after the war. The United States gained much economic power during the war. All of these factors made the gold standard ineffective. The gold standard was abandoned by most countries at the beginning of World War I. In the period between World War I and World War II, another system was in use.

William Strode/Woodfin, Camp

Some of the gold at Fort Knox

Between the wars, a system called the gold exchange system was in use. After most countries left the gold standard at the beginning of World War I, their currencies were allowed to "float" on the international market. When a currency floats, its value in gold is allowed to go up or down in the international money market. This system of floating currencies was the gold exchange system. As a result of this system, many currencies were devalued. That is, their value with respect to gold went down. This caused exchange rates to change a great deal. It was difficult for one country to do business with another country. It was hard for tourists to visit another country because they could not be sure of bringing enough money with them. All in all, it was not a very good system.

During World War II, Great Britain and the United States tried to deal with the problem of an international agreement on money. The two countries tried to set up a formal system that everyone would use to exchange money between countries. The system they set up is usually called the Bretton Woods System. The system got this name from the town in New Hampshire in the United States where the international agreement was signed. The Bretton Woods agreement was signed in 1944. When it was signed, it seemed to be a good system.

The Bretton Woods agreement had two main parts. The first part concerned exchange rates. All of the countries that signed the agreement promised to regulate their exchange rates. The countries promised not to change their exchange rates too often. This was a very important part of the agreement. It helped to stabilize the international finance system. The second part of the Bretton Woods agreement concerned a currency fund. The fund was supposed to help countries that needed currency. All the countries contributed some of their currency to the fund. They could borrow the necessary currency from the fund. This helped all of the member countries to do business with each other. This second part of the agreement was called the International Monetary Fund (IMF).

The Bretton Woods System is still in use. Like the gold standard, it seems better than it really is. There are problems with the Bretton Woods System, too. First, the IMF has no way to make the member countries do what it says. Member countries can still do whatever they want with their own exchange rates. A second problem of the IMF is that it did not set up an international monetary policy that all countries agreed to follow. Each country still has its own monetary policy. A third problem of the IMF is that it cannot deal with special problems. One special problem was the war in Viet Nam. The system could not take care of the monetary problems caused by the war.

Although a new system to regulate international finance is needed, it will be very difficult to set up. Even from this short explanation, it is easy to see how complex the world of international finance is.

EXERCISES
Comprehension
1. What are the two concerns of international finance?
2. What was the gold standard system?

3. How did the gold standard start?
4. Why wasn't the gold standard a good system?
5. Why did most countries go off the gold standard at the beginning of World War I?
6. What system was used between World War I and World War II?
7. What is a floating currency?
8. What happens when a currency is devalued?
9. What is the Bretton Woods System?
10. Why isn't the Bretton Woods System as good as it seems?

Associated Press

Bretton Woods Conference

Discussion
Part A
1. Do you think we should go back to the gold standard? Why or why not?
2. Why would a new international monetary agreement be hard to set up?
3. Is international finance important to you?
   Part B
1. Have you ever had to exchange money? Describe your experience.

Directed Sentences
Directions: Make sentences using the following word groups. You may use any form of a given word. You may use the words in any order.
1. inflation-goods and services-forces-abandoned
2. simple-figure-rates-borrow

3. underlying-trade-policy-finance
4. nationalism-intensely-native
5. gold standard-widely-monetary
6. fund-agency-regulate-stabilize
7. power-gained-bullion
8. contact-foreign-inherently-valuable
9. float-currency-devalued
10. informally-agreement-among

Suggested Reading
Aliber, Robert. *The International Money Game* (Basic Books, 1976)
Smith, Adam. *The Money Game* (Random House, 1976)

FOODS INTERNATIONAL

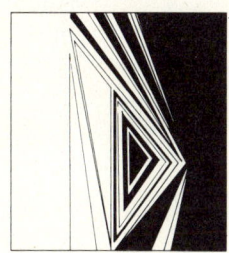 If you visit a big city anywhere in the world, you will probably find a restaurant which serves the food of your native country. Most large cities in the United States offer an international sample of foods. Many people enjoy eating the food of other nations. This is probably one reason why there are so many different kinds of restaurants in the United States. A second reason is that many Americans come from other parts of the world. They enjoy tasting the foods of their native lands. In the city of Detroit, for example, there are many people from Western Europe, Greece, Latin America, and the Far East. There are many restaurants in Detroit which serve the foods of these areas. There are many other international restaurants, too. Americans enjoy the foods in these restaurants as well as the opportunity to better understand the people and their way of life. A few of the international restaurants usually found in most large cities in the United States will be described here.

One of the most common international restaurants to be found in the United States is an Italian restaurant. The restaurant may be a small business run by a single family. The mother of the family cooks all of the dishes and the father and children serve the people who come to eat there. Or it may be a large restaurant which can serve many people during one evening. It may be owned by one family, one person, or by several different people who work together in the business.

Many Italian dishes that Americans enjoy are made with some form of pasta such as spaghetti or lasagna. These are not the only kinds of food Italian people eat. There are many delicious dishes made with veal and other meats. Many of these dishes include tomatoes and cheese and are tasty. All of these dishes are very good.

In Detroit, and many other cities, there are many Greek people. In a section of Detroit there are many Greek shops and restaurants. It is fun to go there for lunch or dinner at a Greek restaurant. There are many Greek restaurants in this section. It is fun to walk down the streets there and smell the many different dishes cooking.

Many Greek dishes are made with lamb. One of these dishes is called moussaka. It is made with lamb, eggplant, and cheese. The lamb is ground up

Mimi Forsyth/Monkmeyer

Rice in Oriental cooking

for this dish, and cooked with the eggplant and cheese. This is a very popular dish. Another favorite with Americans is shish kabob. This is another dish made with lamb, and usually with tomatoes and a vegetable or potato. The lamb is cut into small squares and put on a skewer. The tomatoes and vegetables are also put on the skewer and it is all cooked together. After eating a meal of moussaka or shish kabob, you may not want anything more to eat. However, a Greek pastry called baklava is hard to resist for dessert, even when you are full. It is made with fruit and honey, wrapped in a very thin pastry. It is very good, even when you are full.

In Western Europe and in Greece, many foods are made from wheat. The pastry in baklava is made with wheat flour. Italian pasta is also made from wheat flour. In part of the world, there is a great deal of wheat. It is easy to get and many things are made from it. In some parts of the world, however, wheat is not easy to get. In these parts of the world, many things are made from corn or rice instead of wheat. Mexico is one place where corn is easier to get than wheat. Much corn grows in Mexico, and many things are made from the corn that grows there.

Many Mexican dishes are made with a thin, flat cornmeal cake called a tortilla. Sometimes, the tortillas are eaten by themselves, in much the same way that other people might eat bread. But many Mexican dishes use the tortillas in combination with meat and other things. A taco is one Mexican food of this kind. A taco is made from a corn tortilla, which is folded in half. Inside the tortilla, cooked meat, and uncooked tomatoes, lettuce, and cheese are put together. Then you may put taco sauce on the taco. The sauce is very spicy. Many people enjoy eating tacos, but they have to drink lots of water after they have finished eating this spicy dish.

In Mexico, as you can see, corn meal is used in making tortillas, which are an important part of some dishes. In Europe and in Greece, many things are made with wheat. In the Far East, many things are made with rice instead of corn or wheat. If you go out to eat dinner in any kind of Oriental restaurant, most of the foods will be served with rice. This is true of the various kinds of Chinese and Japanese foods, as well as other Oriental foods.

There are two kinds or styles of Chinese cooking that are popular in the United States. One of these comes from the northern part of China. It is called Mandarin cooking. The other kind of Chinese cooking comes from the south of China. It is called Cantonese style cooking. Most Americans enjoy Cantonese style Chinese food. There are not really very many Mandarin style Chinese restaurants in the United States. Mandarin and Cantonese style Chinese foods are somewhat similar.

In both kinds of Chinese food, the meats and vegetables are cut up and cooked together. Everything is cut up into very small pieces. Usually, a thin, dark liquid is used to flavor the cooking. This liquid is called soy sauce. All of this is true of both Mandarin and Cantonese style foods. However, these two kinds of cooking are also different. Cantonese dishes usually have a heavy sauce.

They are usually served with rice. Mandarin cooking usually has a thin sauce. The meat and vegetable combination is served with rice. Mandarin dishes contain a few spices. They are just a little spicy and taste good, but they are usually not very spicy. You will not be very thirsty after a Mandarin style meal.

Mandarin and Cantonese style Chinese cooking are not the only kinds of Chinese cooking there are. There are many other forms of Chinese cooking. All of them are very good. Chinese food, perhaps because it is so different from American food, is interesting and fun to eat.

Another kind of Oriental food that is interesting to eat is Japanese food. In most Japanese restaurants in the United States, you can get a feeling for the Japanese way of life. You will probably sit on the floor in a Japanese restaurant, and you may be asked to take off your shoes. Usually, Japanese food is cooked right at your table. Everything in your dinner is brought to your table uncooked. The person who serves also cooks your dinner. It is very interesting to watch all of the various parts of the meal get cooked together.

Japanese food is a little like Chinese food. Everything is cut up, but some of the pieces of meat and vegetables are bigger in Japanese food than in Chinese food. Also, Japanese food is almost always served with rice, just like Chinese food. Japanese food may be more like Mandarin style Chinese food because it often has a thin sauce, and is just a little spicy. Sukiyaki, which is made with meat and vegetables which are cooked together, is very good. Other kinds of Japanese food are also very good.

You can find all of these kinds of restaurants in almost every large American city. If you visit the United States, going to one of these restaurants may make you homesick. You will probably enjoy the taste of your native foods just the same.

EXERCISES
Comprehension
1. Give two reasons why there are many international restaurants in the United States.
2. Is an Italian restaurant always a small business owned by one family?
3. What are some Italian dishes Americans enjoy?
4. Describe a Greek section in Detroit.
5. Why do many Mexican dishes use corn meal?
6. What are two styles of Chinese cooking?
7. How are these two styles similar?
8. Is Japanese food like Chinese food? Why or why not?
9. How is Japanese food usually cooked and served?

Discussion
Part A
1. Have you had any of the foods described here? Did you like them or not?
2. Describe one of your favorite dishes.
3. Have you been to an international restaurant? Describe the experience.

Greek section of Detroit

Part B

1. Do you think international restaurants contribute to better understanding between countries? Explain your point of view.
2. Compare two kinds of foods you have had (French and German food, for example). Which did you like best? Why?

Directed Sentences

Directions: Make sentences using the following word groups. You may use any form of a given word. You may use the words in any order.

1. rice-pasta
2. baklava-pastry-honey
3. moussaka-eggplant
4. shish kabob-lamb-skewer
5. Detroit-spaghetti-lasagna-veal
6. taco-tortilla-uncooked-lettuce-tomatoes
7. Cantonese-Mandarin-styles-soy sauce
8. Oriental sukiyaki-homesick
9. spicy-sauce
10. cornmeal-flour

Suggested Reading

Pellegrini, Angelo. *Wine and the Good Life* (Knopf, 1965)
Root, Waverley. *The Food of Italy* (Random House, 1977)
Tannahill, Reay. *Food in History* (Stein and Day, 1974)
Gourmet magazine

ON
MARRIAGE
An Opinion

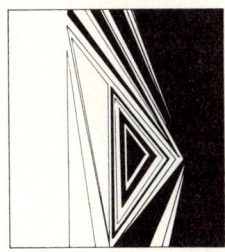 Whether you are married or not, you probably have some opinion on marriage. Perhaps you think marriage is a good idea. Perhaps you are already married, and you are very happy. Or you may think that marriage is a very bad idea. If you are married, perhaps you are not happy. If you are single, perhaps you would rather live alone. The writer believes that marriage is a good thing. There are several reasons and feelings underlying this belief.

There are three reasons why marriage seems to be a good idea. The first of these reasons has to do with the American way of life. In general, many Americans think that marriage is good. Many young people expect to get married. American society expects that many people will get married. However, a number of people do not marry. There are a number of reasons for this. Perhaps you have never met anyone you wanted to marry. Perhaps you would rather be single than be in an average marriage. Perhaps you simply do not think that marriage is a good thing. In spite of these reasons that some people have not to marry, most people in the United States expect to marry.

A second reason why marriage can be good has to do with children. Many married couples have children. The writer believes that a married couple is in a good position to have children and to raise them successfully. Many people would disagree with this idea. The writer thinks that a family made up of a mother, a father, and children is the best situation for raising happy, healthy children. Some people think that children ought to be shared among several sets of parents. They like the idea of three or four couples taking the responsibility for all of their children. Then the children are exposed to several sets of parents. This may be a good idea, but it is very new to the writer. The writer still believes that one set of parents is best qualified to raise its own children.

A third reason why marriage seems good has to do with finances. Married people may have fewer problems with money. Usually, the husband works to earn the money for the family's expenses. Sometimes the wife works instead of the husband. Sometimes, both husband and wife work. In any of these situations, the family will have at least one person earning enough money for their expenses. This is a very good situation to be in. Of course, many married couples have

Parents and child

money problems. Sometimes a person will lose a job even though he or she has done nothing wrong. Sometimes a family will not earn enough money for all its expenses, because of illness or other extra expenses. Many people have money problems. The writer believes that married people have a better chance to work out these problems than single people do. Many banks and other places where you can borrow money feel the same way. They make it easier for married people to borrow money than for single people to borrow. In general, married people usually have a better monetary situation.

The writer also has some feelings about marriage. These feelings are not things that you can analyze. They are the writer's feelings, and you may agree or disagree with them, but you cannot prove them. The writer feels that marriage can be good because of the feelings of love, understanding, and fun.

The feeling of love is essential to a marriage. If two people do not love each other, they probably should not be married. Marriage can be good for two people who love each other. If you love another person, you probably want to be with that person all the time, or as much as possible. Marriage provides you with a way of doing this. If you are married, you may live with the person you love. You and your spouse can be together most of the time.

Marriage can keep you from feeling alone. When you feel that you are alone, you may feel that you have no friends, and that no one cares about you. If you are married, you know that there is always someone living with you who cares about you. In a good marriage, no one is really alone. It is nice to know that even when your life does not seem to go very well, someone will always love you and take care of you.

Marriage can also be good because of a feeling of understanding. Not only does your spouse care for you and help you, but you also care for and help your spouse. If your spouse has trouble with a job, or some friends, or family problems, you may be able to help him or her solve these problems. Then your spouse may be able to help you with some problem of yours. You can both help each other in this way. This is a very good part of marriage, and it is helpful to many people who are married. It is also true that sometimes your spouse can help you just by listening to your problems. Neither of you may be able to solve the problems. However, you will feel better if you can talk about them with someone who loves and understands you.

Finally, marriage can be good because it can be fun. You can be with someone you love almost all the time. You can do things together, talk to each other, and generally enjoy yourselves being together. It is possible to have a lot of fun as a married person. Of course, it is possible to have a lot of fun as a single person, too. Some people might say that you can have more fun as a single person. The writer thinks it is much more fun to be married.

These are some of the feelings that the writer has about marriage and the reasons for them. You may not agree with any of them, or only with some. Your opinion is completely up to you. The writer thinks that marriage can be good, and has tried to explain why.

EXERCISES

Comprehension

1. What does the writer think about marriage?
2. What do most Americans think about marriage?
3. Why are some adults not married?
4. What is the second reason the writer thinks that marriage is good?
5. Why is it sometimes true that married people have fewer money problems?
6. Why is it easier for married people to borrow money?
7. What is the difference between reasons and feelings?
8. What feelings does the writer have about marriage?
9. Explain why understanding is important to a marriage.
10. Why is marriage fun?

Discussion

Part A

1. What is the writer's opinion about marriage?
2. Find a few sentences in the reading where the writer's reasons for this opinion are stated.
3. Find a few sentences in the reading where the writer's feelings are given.

Part B

1. How do you feel about marriage? Why?
2. What would it be like to live in a society where there was no marriage?
3. Are you married? If you are, do you think marriage is a good thing? If you are not, do you want to get married?
4. Explain how most people in your country feel about marriage.

Several adults caring for a child

Suggested Reading
Casler, Lawrence. *Is Marriage Necessary?* (Human Science Press, 1974)
O'Neill, Nena, and George O'Neill. *Open Marriage: A New Life Style for Couples*
  (Avon, 1973)
Rogers, Carl. *Becoming Partners: Marriage and Its Alternatives* (Delacorte, 1972)

WORD STUDY REVIEW

To the student: These exercises will help you to learn new words in English
more easily. Study each part carefully, and review new words from the first
twenty-four chapters.

A. Noun ending: **-ence**
    The ending *-ence* is added to words to make nouns meaning "act," "state,"
    or "result." Add the ending *-ence* to the following words from the first
    twenty-four chapters.
    confide-confid_____   refer-refer_____
    differ-differ_____   violent-viol_____

B. Noun ending: **-ity**
    The ending *-ity* is added to words to make nouns meaning "state" or
    "quality." Add the ending *-ity* to the following words from the first twenty-
    four chapters.
    able-abil_____   opportune-opportun_____
    equal-equal_____   popular-popular_____
    immune-immun_____   responsible-responsibil_____
                             similar-similar_____

C. Adjective ending: **-ive**
    The ending *-ive* is added to words to make adjectives meaning "of," "having
    the nature of," or "tending to." Add the ending *-ive* to the following words
    from the first twenty-four chapters:
    affirm-affirmat_____   effect-effect_____
    explode-explos_____   represent-representat_____

D. **Usage Practice**
    Directions: Fill in the blank with the correct form of the word given in brackets
    [ ].
    1. Many women have a great deal of [confide] _____ in themselves.
    2. [Affirm] _____ action is helpful to women and other minority groups.
    3. Marriage, for many people, is an important [responsible] _____.
    4. Equal [opportune] _____ is important for everyone.
    5. The [popular] _____ of baseball in America is really great.
    6. There are many [similar] _____ between soccer and rugby.
    7. In the library you must go to the [refer] _____ desk or area.
    8. There is too much [violent] _____ on American television.
    9. Many women have the [able] _____ to do important jobs.
    10. Dynamite is only one kind of [explode] _____ material.

GLOSSARY

The following glossary is made up of the vocabulary given special study in each chapter. As no new vocabulary is introduced in the Opinion Papers (chapters 5, 10, 15, 20, and 25), these chapters are not included here.

Higher Education in the United States   *1*

Adults   grown persons

Amount   number—the same amount means the same number of years here

Associate of Arts or Science degree   the level reached after two years of study after high school

Auto mechanics   the subject of fixing cars

Bachelor of Arts or Science degree   the level reached after four years of study after high school. (B.A. or B.S.)

Carpentry   the subject of building and repairing things made of wood

Charity organization   a group of people who help other people who are in trouble

Community   an area or small town where people live

Contribution   money or other help given to people or a business or other place

Dental technology   the subject of helping care for peoples' teeth

Described   told about something

Diploma   a document given to students who have completed high school to show that they have completed the requirements

Electronics   the subject of building or fixing things like radios and televisions

Enter   to come or go into

Equivalent   the same as

Expenses   the amount of money needed

Graduate   the level reached after four years of study after high school. A person with a B.A. or B.S. is a graduate

Grandchildren   children of your son or daughter

Group   a number of people or things that are the same in some way

Higher education   all kinds of education after high school in the United States

However   but
Humanities   areas of study having to do with human thinking
Investments   the money that is put into a business to get more money
Larger   bigger
Liberal arts   the following subjects are liberal arts subjects: literature, philosophy, history, languages, art, music, and others
Nonacademic   not usually school subjects
Others   ones not talked about
Plumbing   the subject of fixing water pipes
Private   owned by a person or a few people, rather than by the government
Professional   a person who is a doctor, dentist, lawyer, or in another group where much study is necessary
Publicly funded   money for expenses comes from the government
Receives   gets
Sewing   the subject of making clothes
Sources   places or people from which information or money may be gotten
Technical or vocational   kinds of schools where people can learn to do a job
Trade union   a group of people who work together to get better jobs, better pay, and other things
Training   learning to do something
Tuition   money paid by students to a school
Undergraduate degree   same as a B.A. or B.S.
University   a group of schools and colleges giving B.A., B.S., and graduate or professional degress

Linguistics   7
Ability   being able to
Account   explain
Actually   really
Allow   let
Ambiguous   having more than one meaning
Believe   think or take something to be true or real
Certain   specific, but not named
Chicken   a bird that people eat
Concerned   was about or relative to
Easier   more easy than
Field   area of study
Infinite   very large
Knowledge   all the things that you know
Linguist   a person interested in language
Linguistics   the study of man's language
Meaning   the ideas
Native language   the language you learned as a child, spoken by your family, in your country

Person   one man or woman
Possibility   something that can be or happen
Professor   a teacher in college or at a university
Scholar   a man or woman who studies a lot
Speaker   a man or woman who uses a language
Theory   an idea or guess about something that has not been proven
Transformational generative grammar   an idea about how people know and use
      language
Unused   not used

The Olympics   13

Achievements   things done very well by a person
Affect   to have an effect on
Amateur   one who does something for fun, not for money
Athletes   persons with training in games and activities
Catch   to get in your hands
Century   one hundred years
Chance   probability
Committee   a group of people who work together to reach a goal
Compete   to play games
Competition   playing games to win
Contests   games
Decision   the act of deciding on a question
Effect   change in some way
Entries   persons in some activities
Events   particular, games in the Olympics
Excellent   the best
Greatest   the most important
Gymnastics   activities to train the body
History   the story of what has happened in the past
Hit   to strike one thing with another
Individual   a single person, working alone
Jumping   springing or rising from the ground
Kick   to strike with your foot
Limits   the place where something ends
Meeting   a group of people who get together for a particular reason
Mentioned   talked about
Political   about a government of a country
Race   a game where the fastest person or group wins
Relay   a kind of race where each person goes part of the distance
Representative   a person or thing which stands for something else
Represented   stood for
Score   the number of points gotten by a team
Skiing   gliding over snow on long pieces of wood on the feet
Soccer   a game played like football, using a round ball

Sports   active games people play
Strict   keeping the rules fully
Stronger   more able in some activity
Suggested   proposed an idea
Times   an era in the past or present
Types   kinds or varieites
Volleyball   a team game played by hitting a large ball over a net with the hands
Win   succeed

Male/Female Roles in the United States   19

Bills   pieces of paper showing how much money you must give for something you have bought
Choice   a variety from which to choose
Comfortable   at ease or happy
Cooked   made ready to eat
Divorce   lawful end of a marriage
Factory   a building where things are made
Form   a way of doing something
Household   a home and all the people in it
Impressions   ideas that are not specific
Institution   a way of doing something that has been used for a long time
Marriage   the state of being husband and wife
Married   being husband and wife
Occurred   happened
Relationships   connections between people
Responsibilities   jobs and other things that must be done
Reverse   exchange
Role   not often a way of acting
Seldom   not often
Society   a group of people. In this essay, all Americans
Somewhere   in, to, or at some place
Spouse   husband or wife
Traditional   acting the same way people have for a long time

Television   31

Advertising   publicly describing something so that people will buy it
Afford   be able to buy
Annoying   bothering
Aspects   views of a thing or idea
Boring   not interesting
Channels   TV stations
Companies   businesses
Complaint   a statement that you are unhappy about something
Conversations   talks between two people or a small group

Cry   make noise and show fears

Deliberately   slowly and on purpose

Development   events resulting from growth or improvement

Discussed   talked about

Dislike   not like

Educational   helpful to learning

Entertaining   enjoyable, fun

Feelings   opinions

Health   the state of your body

Industry   a business that makes and sells things

Inform   to give knowledge

Interview   talk with

Laugh   the sound you make when you are having fun

Learn   know from studying, reading, or listening

Literature   very good writing

Local   having to do with a small area

Misleading   not right

Noncommercial   not commercial—not making money

Ought   should

Politics   the science of government

Possible   can be or happen, but may not

Product   something made by someone

Realistic   like life or facts

Refuse   say no to the idea of doing something

Series   on TV, a number of programs with the same people or about one thing

Solve   find the answer; explain

Sponsored   paid for

Technology   applied science

Unsophisticated   not complex

Upset   unhappy or bothered

Various   several different kinds

Violence   hurting someone or something

Violent   acting to hurt someone or something

The Stock Market   37

Advantageous   good

Bank   a place where money is kept

Basically   mainly or mostly

Broker   a person who is allowed to buy and sell stock

Dividend   an amount of money divided among owners of a stock

Gamble   a chance taken

"Go public"   be part of a stock exchange—a company that goes public may sell shares at the exchange

Guarantee   promise

In general   usually; not always

In hopes of   hoping

Invest   put money into a business, in order to get more money

Investor   a person who tries to make money through investments

Issues   gives out or sends

Licensed   allowed by law to do something

Manufacturing   making things

Market   a place where people get together to exchange things and money

Order   asking for something

Owe   have to give someone or something (like a bank) some money

Ownership   possession of something

Partial   some, but not all

Plus   in addition

Price   the amount of money asked or given for something

Profit   money left after all bills are paid

Raise   increase in amount

Save   keep for future use

Sell   give in exchange for money

Shares   parts

Somewhat   a little

Stock   parts of a company which may be bought or sold

Stock exchange   the place where people buy or sell parts of companies

Tax   money a person or business must pay to the government

True   factual; real

Wealthy   having a large amount of money

Women in Sports   43

Academic   having to do with school or college

Arenas   places where sports competition is held

Available   easily found

Case   (the case) the way things are

Championships   contests to find out who is best

Collegiate   of or like a college student

Considered   thought of or about

Delicacy   not strong, but very fine

Encourages   helps

Explanation   a meaning

Frailty   easily broken or weak

General   of, for, or from all. Not special

Golf   a game played outside with a small, hard ball and a set of long tools called clubs. The goal of the game is to hit the ball into a number of small holes with the smallest number of hits.

Growing   increasing

Illness   sickness. Not healthy.

Image   the idea or representation of something
Involve   become part of
Join   become part of a group or team
Member   a person who is part of a group or team
National   having to do with a whole country
Noted   mentioned
Noticeable   most easy to see
Participate   have or take part in some activity
Participation   sharing in some activity
Players   people who play a sport or game
Popularity   being liked by many people
Regarded   thought of as important or especially good
Serious   important
Simply   in a way that is not complex
Steadily   regularly or always the same
Substantially   in the main; mostly; largely
Tennis   a game in which players hit a small ball over a net using tools called rackets
Track   running, jumping, and other activities
Unladylike   not refined
Victorian   characteristic of the time when Victoria was queen of England (1839–1901)
Within   on the inside

History of Biology   *49*

Belonged to   be a part of
Binomial nomenclature   a way of naming something by using a two-part name
Biologists   people who study the science of plants and animals
Biology   the science that deals with plants and animals
Botanical   having to do with plants
Botany   the science that deals with plants; part of biology
Classified   put in groups
Collectors   people who put things together in a large group and save them
Discoveries   findings of new things
Evolution   the development of plants or animals through centuries
Explorer   a person who travels to new places
Extremely   very greatly
Fairly   generally
Genus   a general group of plants or animals
Improved   made better
Lenses   pieces of glass used to help in seeing
Magnifying   making larger
Microscopists   people who used a microscope, a tool which made very small things look much larger
Observation   the result of looking at something

Observer   a person who looks at things
Reference   a source of information
Renaissance   a time when many people in Europe became interested in art and learning—14th, 15th, and 16th centuries
Samples   examples
Species   a particular kind of plant or animal
System   an organization
Systematize   put in some order
Unaware   not aware; not knowing

The Nobel Prize   61

Academy   a group of people who work in a particular area of thought or science
Award   give something, or the thing that is given
Background   information about the past
Caroline Medical Institute   a group of people who work in medicine in Stockholm
Chemist   a person who works in chemistry
Chemistry   the science of what things are made of
Deserve   be good enough to get something
Detonators   things which make other things explode
Diplomats   people who represent their government in talks with others
Dynamite   material that makes things explode
Explosives   materials that make things blow up. Dynamite is one kind of explosive.
Great   much above average
Honor   something given to someone for something highly regarded
Invent   think up or make something that is new
Inventions   new things
Inventor   a person who makes new things
Medal   a small flat piece, usually of gold, given to someone for an achievement
Negotiations   talks between people or countries to try to solve problems
Nominate   name someone for some job or some present
Nomination   the process of naming someone (as above)
Nominee   a person named by nomination
Outstanding   much better than others
Peace   when there is no war
Physics   the science of how things act
Physiology   the study of human life processes
Poet   a person who writes poems
Prestige   high regard as the result of high achievement
Prize   something given for high achievement
Recommendation   saying something good about someone
Reward   something given in exchange for something done
Royal Academy of Science   a group of people who work in science in Stockholm
Trust fund   money held by a group of people for another person
Whether   if it is the case
Winner   a person who is the best

Animal Language   67

Amaze   do something wonderful
Bee   a small insect that feeds on flowers
Behavior   how a person acts.
Circle   a round shape
Combinations   things put together
Combine   join or bring things together
Communicate   give or get information
Computer   a machine which can do many things electronically
Correct   right
Definition   the meaning of a word or idea
Dolphin   a large kind of fish in the ocean
Generalize   figure out in general from particular examples
Hive   a home for bees
Intelligent   bright, able to think well
Monkey   an animal very similar to man, but smaller and less bright
Similarity   being like someone or something, but not the same
Smell   know by using your nose
Speech   talking
Speed   how fast something or someone goes
Symbols   things that represent other things
Tail-wagging   moving the tail or end of the body
Throat   the front part of the neck
Wiggle   move from side to side
Yerkes Primate Research Center   an institution in the state of Georgia (in the United States) where monkeys are studied by scientists

News Sources   73

Actions   behavior
Besides   also or added to
Candidate   a person running for a job in government
Cause   bring about
Contain   have in it or to hold
Criticize   state the bad points about something
Daily   every day
Davis Cup   a championship in tennis
Editorial   an essay in which a person who works for a newspaper gives his or her opinion on a subject
Editors   people who work for a newspaper
Election   choosing by vote
Features   stories in the newspaper that are not about the news
Fix   repair
Folded   a single piece of something arranged so that one half of it touches the other half of it

Helpful   giving help
Include   have as part
Influence   have an effect on
Informative   giving information
Leaders   people who are heads of groups
Lower   smaller in amount or number
Main   the most important
Major   very important
Nearby   near; not far away
No matter   regardless of
On sale   available for less money
Particular   specific
Practice   do something many times until you can do it well
Printed   made by a press
Qualified   able to do a job
Useful   something that can be used
World Cup   a championship in soccer

Dating Patterns in the USA   79

Admission   the price for going in to a movie, game, etc.
Baseball   a game played with a small ball by two teams on a field with four bases
Coffee house   a small restaurant where coffee is served
Common   usual
Cost   the price of something
Couple   two people. Usually, a boy and a girl or a man and a woman
Differ   be different from
Drawbacks   bad points
Formal   within social rules, socially correct
Freedom   being able to act any way you want to
Lead to   make something happen
Night   the hours after sunset and before sunrise
Night club   a restaurant for drinking, dancing, and fun
Pair   to put into groups of two people or things
Patterns   characteristic behavior
Pay   give money in exchange for
Relax   rest
Respect   (with respect to)—in relationship to

Lasers   93

Beam   a thin stream of light
Cell   a very small part of a living thing such as a plant or animal
Communications   the sending and getting of information
Concentrate   to increase the strength of something

Conditions   states of being at a particular time
Continuous   not stopping
Control   check or hold back
Device   a machine
Drilling   digging in the ground
Energy   power or force
Fiber optics   the field of working with lasers to keep them from being damaged
Focus   bring together at a single point
Gas   matter in a form which can expand
(to) Heat   to make hot
Hurricanes   storms with rains and winds
Laser   a machine which makes a special kind of light
Lay down   put in the ground
Liquid   anything like water
Measurement   the result of measuring something
Pipeline   line of long, thin, hollow material through which water, oil, or other things can be sent
Powerful   very strong
Predict   tell in advance
Processes   ways of doing something
Produce   make
Protect   prevent from being hurt
Satellite   a machine in space
Signals   signs sent by broadcasting
Surgery   the practice of operating to help people who are sick
Tube   a thin hollow material through which something can be sent

The Stock Market, II   99

Barometer   a tool to help predict the weather, or, anything that marks change
Confidence   believing in someone or something
Crises   very important events (plural of *crisis*)
Dow Jones   three averages of different kinds of stocks
Economic   about a government's money
Economy   the use of money by a government and/or people
Extra   more than is needed or usual
Favorably   liked, felt good about
Flashed   seen for a short time
Index   a sign of
Industrial   having to do with businesses that make and sell things
Largest   the most large
Outlook   point of view
Position   place
Previous   happening or going before

Prosper   do well
Railroad   train
Reaction   feeling or opinion about something
Reflect   give back an image of something
Report   tell about or explain
Strong   heavy in effect
Surprise   take unawares
Trade agreements   treaties which allow two countries to exchange products
Utility   a business that gives something useful, such as water, to people
Wire services   news reports sent by telegram

Three Kinds of Football   105

Arrangement   the way things are arranged
Association football   soccer
British Empire   the group of countries formerly controlled by Britain
Champion   the best
Complicated   complex
Defense   the group defending the goal
Difference   the way in which people or things are not alike
Equal   the same
Except   leaving out
Goal   scoring points
Goalie   the person defending the goal
Half-time   a rest period between two halves of a game
Occasional   not very often
Offense   the group attacking the goal
Once   one time
Opponent   the other team
Opportunity   good chance
Oppose   be against (a team or an idea)
Origins   beginnings
Oval   like an egg
Prevent   stop or keep from doing
Rugby   a team sport played in Great Britain and other countries
Rugby League   professional rugby
Rugby Union   amateur rugby
Settle   go somewhere and live there for a long time
Shape   the form or description of a thing
Specialize   work on one thing or area
Strategy   a plan for doing something
Touch   put one thing next to another so that there is no space between them
Unique   different; not like anything else
Worth   numerical or money value of a thing

Learning a Language   113

Disagree   not agree

Easily   in an easy or simple way

Efforts   tries at doing something

Environment   the area around a person

Exposure   being exposed

Foreign language   some language other than the one you learned as a child

Memorize   go over something many times until you can remember it

Method   a way of doing something

Psychologists   persons who study man's thinking and behavior

Quickly   fast or in a small amount of time

Rare   not usual, not common

Second language   some language other than the one you learned as a child

Similar   alike

Sounds   noises of language

Successful   having a good result

Usage   the way in which language is used

Recent History of Medicine   *125*

Antibiotics   medicines which help you get well when you are sick

Bacteria   small living things, some of which make you sick

Chemicals   materials made by chemists

Chemotherapy   the use of medicines to help you get well when you are sick

Cure   to make a person well or healthy

Diabetes   an illness caused by not being able to use sugar correctly in the body

Disease   an illness

Drugs   medicines

Endocrine   having to do with special materials in your body, made inside your body

Endocrinology   the study of special materials in your body, and the parts of the body that make them

Fungi   small living things, plants (plural of *fungus*)

Germ   a small living thing which causes disease

Germ-free   having no small living things, without germs

Glands   parts of the body which do special work to keep you healthy

Hormones   materials made by some parts of the body

Immunity   the ability to resist an illness

Immuno-deficiency   disease of not having any immunities

Immunology   the study of the ability to resist illness

Ineffective   not effective, not having any effect

Injection   the giving of medicine by making it go into the body through a special tool

Insulin   a material made by part of the body and needed to use sugar

Kidney   a part of the body that filters out body wastes

Lack   to be without; to have none of something

Microorganisms   small living things

Oral contraceptive pill   a medicine taken by mouth to prevent a women from having a child

Organ a part of the body
Pancreas a part of the body that helps your body use the food you eat
Penicillin a medicine which helps you get well when you have certain illnesses
Pneumonia a serious disease of the lungs
Polio a very serious illness
Reject to not be able or willing to take or use something
Sex hormones materials made by the body which are different in men and women
Smallpox a very serious illness
Sulfa drugs medicines which help you get well when you are sick
Transplant taking from one place and putting in another
Treat to try to make a person better when he is sick
Typhoid a very serious illness
Vaccines materials that keep you from getting some illnesses

Women's Liberation *131*
Accomplish to succeed in doing
Affirmative Action a law which encourages businesses to give women and minority groups a fair chance
Attitudes feelings on a particular subject
Beliefs opinions
Capable able to do something
Career a job
Cure to make free of illness
Entitled having a right to
Equality the state of being equal or the same
Fellow workers other people a person works with
Goal a purpose
Identity the fact of being a particular person or thing
Issues problems; points being questioned
Liberation freedom
Minority group a group of people fewer in number and different from the main group
Movement a group of people working for a single goal
Permit to allow
Profession a field of work
Qualified filling the needs of a job
Respected treated with honor

International Finance *137*
Abandoned gave up completely
Agency an office of a business
Agreement an understanding between people or nations
Among in the group of
Borrow take something with the promise to return it
Bullion plain gold

Contact in touch with
Currency money
Devalued having less value
Figure add up
Finance having to do with money
Float move about freely
Forces causes
Foreign not of your own country
Fund some money set aside for some reason
Gained got
Gold standard a money system in which all money was valued in terms of gold
Goods and services things, and things done for other people
Inflation when there is too much money in a country and prices go up
Informally not formal
Inherently natural part of a person or thing
Intensely very strongly
Monetary having to do with money
Nationalism a strong feeling for your own country
Native connected with the country you were born in
Policy a plan for government of something
Power influence over other people, countries, etc.
Rates prices
Regulate control
Simple easy
Stabilize keep from changing
Trade business
Underlying forming the basis of
Valuable having value
Widely over a large area

Foods International 143
Baklava a kind of Greek dessert
Cantonese a kind of Chinese food
Cornmeal a kind of flour made from corn
Detroit a large city in the state of Michigan, in the United States
Eggplant a kind of vegetable
Flour finely ground meal of a cereal grain
Homesick longing or wishing for home
Honey a sugar-like part of some foods
Lamb a kind of meat
Lasagna an Italian food made with meat, cheese, and other things
Lettuce a plant used in salad and other dishes
Mandarin a kind of Chinese food
Moussaka a kind of Greek food
Oriental coming from or having to do with the Far East (China, Japan, etc.)

Pasta   any of several wheat and egg foods of Italian origin

Pastry   a kind of dessert

Rice   a kind of basic food grown where the weather is warm

Sauce   a liquid served with food

Shish kabob   a Greek dish

Skewer   a long, thin tool used to hold food for cooking

Soy sauce   liquid used with Oriental foods

Spaghetti   an Italian dish

Spicy   having a strong taste

Styles   kinds or types

Sukiyaki   a Japanese dish

Taco   a Mexican dish

Tomatoes   a kind of fruit used in salad, tacos, and many other things

Tortilla   a corn meal cake which is round and flat

Uncooked   not cooked, raw

Veal   a kind of meat